D0883996

To Juliska

Gyorgy Kepes

language of vision

With introductory essays by **S. GIEDION** and **S. I. HAYAKAWA**

Paul Theobald 1951

Acknowledgements

First of all the author wishes to acknowledge his indebtedness to the Gestalt psychologists. Many of the inspiring ideas and concrete illustrations of Max Whertheimer, K. Koffka, and W. Kohler, have been used in the first part of the book to explain the laws of visual organization.

The author also acknowledges his gratitude to his publisher, his students, his colleagues, and his friends, for their encouragement and generous help in solving the many creative and technical problems related to this book.

Adeline Cross, Britton Harris, Ann Horn, Eva Manzardo, R. B. Tague, and Mollie Thwaites, and particularly Katinka Loeser and Helen Van de Woestyne gave invaluable aid in the painstaking work of revising and reformulating the text. The author wishes also to thank Professors Charles Morris and S. I. Hayakawa who read the manuscript and gave helpful criticisms.

It would have been an arduous, if not an impossible, task to illustrate this book properly without the help of the students of the author, his colleagues, and the members of the staffs of leading museums. To these the author and the publisher wish to express their sincere gratitude. Our special thanks are due to Miss Frances Pernas of the Museum of Modern Art for her unfailing courtesies; to Frank Levstik, Jr., and Hans Richter for their efforts; to Carl O. Schniewind and Walter J. Sherwood of the Art Institute of Chicago; to Peggy Guggenheim of the Art of this Century; to Baroness Rebay of the Solomon R. Guggenheim Foundation; to J. B. Lippincott & Co., Charles Downs of Abbott Laboratories for the loan of several engravings; to Egbert Jacobson of Container Corporation of America, Harry Collins of Collins, Miller, and Hutchings, R. D. Middleton and Dr. R. L. Leslie for their aid with illustrations and for their contributions of engravings.

Contents

This book, written by a young artist, bears witness that a third generation is on the march, willing to continue and to make secure the modern tradition which has developed in the course of this century; or, as Gyorgy Kepes states it: "To put earlier demands into concrete terms and on a still wider social plane."

It was not the rule in the nineteenth century for younger generations to consciously continue the work of their predecessors. To do so is new; it means that we are in a period of consolidation.

The public, including those who govern and administer it, is still lacking the artistic, that is, the emotional training corresponding to our period. Both are plagued by the split which exists between advanced methods of thinking and an emotional background that has not caught up with these methods. The demand for continuity will become more and more the key word of this period. 'Every day something new' is the inheritance of the last century's disastrous urge. It still persists in many ways. Continuity does not mean standstill or reaction. Continuity means development. Every period changes, as the body does, from day to day. Gothic, Renaissance, Baroque were, in all their phases, constantly developing. But these changes have to be rooted in other than purely materialistic considerations. They have to grow from other sources: the medieval Kingdom of God, the absolutism of the seventeenth century, a political faith, or even an artistic credo.

'Every day something new' reveals helplessness combined with lack of inner conviction, and always eager to flatter the worst instincts of the public. It means change for change's sake, change for the sake of high-pressure salesmanship. It means demoralization.

Public taste today is formed mainly by publicity and the articles of daily use. By these it can be educated or corrupted. Responsible are the art directors in industry and advertising firms and the buyers for department- 5 & 10 and drugstores, who act as censors and level down the designs of the artists to their own conception of the public's taste. They are supposed to feed the assembly line in the speediest way and as a safeguard they judge the public taste lower than it really is. Their educational responsibility seems to have no claim to existence.

Who still believes that art, modern art, has to be defined as a mere luxury or something far-away, remote from real life, unworthy of the respect of a 'doer,' had better not touch this book. Gyorgy Kepes, as we all do, regards art as indispensable to a full life. His main object is to demonstrate just how the optical revolution—around 1910—formed our present-day conception of space and the visual approach to reality. He shows how this development was differentiated in many ways of expression, from cubism to surrealism, forming together the multi-faced image of this period. He shows why modern artists had to reject a slavish obedience to the portrayal of objects, why they hated the "trompe-l'oeuil."

The different movements have a common denominator: a new spatial conception. They are not outmoded when they become silent. Each of them is living in us. Step by step, Kepes follows the liberation of the plastic elements: lines, planes, and colors, and the creation of a world of forms of our own. The spatial conception interconnects the meaning fragments and binds them together just as in another period perspective did when it used a single station point for naturalistic representation. We have to note the great care with which Gyorgy Kepes shows the contact of modern art with reality, and how paintings which, at first sight, seem remote from life, are extracted from its very bloodstream.

This book seems to be addressed to the young generation which must re- build America. This rebuilding will be realized only in future years. But the book could have an immediate influence if those who command public taste in the many fields of present-day life would take time on a quiet week-end to read its pages and think it over.

New York, June 12, 1944.   *S. Giedion*

Whatever may be the language one happens to inherit, it is at once a tool and a trap. It is a tool because with it we order our experience, matching the data abstracted from the flux about us with linguistic units: words, phrases, sentences. What is true of verbal languages is also true of visual "languages": we match the data from the flux of visual experience with image-clichés, with stereotypes of one kind or another, according to the way we have been taught to see.

And having matched the data of experience with our abstractions, visual or verbal, we manipulate those abstractions, with or without further reference to the data, and make systems with them. Those systems of abstractions, artefacts of the mind, when verbal, we call "explanations," or "philosophies"; when visual, we call them our "picture of the world."

With these little systems in our heads we look upon the dynamism of the events around us, and we find, or persuade ourselves that we find, correspondences between the pictures inside our heads and the world without. Believing those correspondences to be real, we feel at home in what we regard as a "known" world.

In saying why our abstractions, verbal or visual, are a tool, I have already intimated why they are also a trap. If the abstractions, the words, the phrases, the sentences, the visual clichés, the interpretative stereotypes, that we have inherited from our cultural environment are adequate to their task, no problem is presented. But like other instruments, languages select, and in selecting what they select, they leave out what they do not select. The thermometer, which speaks one kind of limited language, knows nothing of weight. If only temperature matters and weight does not, what the thermometer "says" is adequate. But if weight, or color, or odor, or factors other than temperature matter, then those factors that the thermometer cannot speak about are the teeth of the trap. Every language, like the language of the thermometer, leaves work undone for other languages to do.

It is no accident historically that Mr. Kepes and other artists of similar orientation speak of "the new vision" and the "language of vision." Revisions of language are needed. Every day we are, all of us, as persons, as groups, as societies, caught in the teeth of what the older languages leave completely out of account. We talk of a new, shrunken, interdependent world in the primitive smoke-signals of "nationality," "race," and "sovereignty." We talk of the problems of an age of international cartels and patent monopolies in the economic baby-talk of Poor Richard's Almanack. We attempt to visualize the eventfulness of a universe that is an electrodynamic plenum in the representational clichés evolved at a time when statically-conceived, isolable "objects" were regarded as occupying positions in an empty and absolute "space." Visually, the majority of us are still " 'object'-minded" and not "relation-minded." We are the prisoners of ancient orientations imbedded in the languages we have inherited.

The language of vision determines, perhaps even more subtly and thoroughly than verbal language, the structure of our consciousness. To see in limited modes of vision is not to see at all—to be bounded by the narrowest parochialisms of feeling.

What Mr. Kepes would have us do, then, by his attempt at visual re-education, is to compel us to take into consideration the "refraction" of our inherited modes of vision. This he does by showing us what goes into visual experience. He gives us the "grammar" and the "syntax" of vision: what interplays of what forces in the human nervous system and in the world outside it produce what visual tensions and resolutions of tensions; what combinations of visual elements result in what new organizations of feeling; what "visual statements," apart from "literary" or representational content, can be made with line, color, form, texture, and arrangement.

Purposely depriving us of the easy comfort of all aesthetic stereotypes and interpretative clichés, Mr. Kepes would have us experience vision as vision. Mr. Kepes's endeavor may perhaps best be characterized by the following analogy. To a Chinese scholar, the pleasure to be derived from an inscription is only partly due to the sentiments it may express. He may take delight in the calligraphy even when the inscription is meaningless to him as text. Suppose now a singularly obtuse Chinese scholar existed who was solely preoccupied with the literary or moral content of inscriptions, and totally blind to their calligraphy. How would one ever get him to see the

9

calligraphic qualities of an inscription if he persisted, every time the inscription was brought up for examination, in discussing its literary content, its accuracy or inaccuracy as statement of fact, his approval or disapproval of its moral injunctions?

It is just such a problem that faces the contemporary artist, confronted with a public to whom the literary, sentimental, moral, etc., content of art is art—to whom visual experience as such is an almost completely ignored dimension. The vast majority of us—and by us I mean not only those who profess to know something about "art" but also the general public that delights in magazine covers and insurance company calendars and hunting prints and sailboat pictures—are sophisticated by our cultural environment beyond the point where it is possible easily to understand what people like Mr. Kepes are driving at. We have all been taught, in looking at pictures, to look for too much. Something of the quality of a child's delight in playing with colors and shapes has to be restored to us before we learn to see again, before we unlearn the terms in which we ordinarily see.

This restoration of vision, then, is what Mr. Kepes's "grammar" of vision would accomplish for us.

The revision of the language of vision is not, of course, an artistic end-in-itself for Mr. Kepes. How we deal with reality is determined at the moment of impact by the way in which we grasp it. Vision shares with speech the distinction of being the most important of the means by which we apprehend reality.

To cease looking at things atomistically in visual experience and to see relatedness means, among other things, to lose in our social experience, as Mr. Kepes argues, the deluded self-importance of absolute "individualism" in favor of social relatedness and interdependence. When we structuralize the primary impacts of experience differently, we shall structuralize the world differently.

The reorganization of our visual habits so that we perceive not isolated "things" in "space," but structure, order, and the relatedness of events in space-time, is perhaps the most profound kind of revolution possible—a revolution that is long overdue not only in art, but in all our experience.

S. I. Hayakawa

Illinois Institute of Technology

The Language of Vision

Today we experience chaos. The waste of human and material resources and the canalization of almost all creative effort into blind alleys bear witness to the fact that our common life has lost its coherency. In the focus of this eclipse of a healthy human existence is the individual, torn by the shattered fragments of his formless world, incapable of organizing his physical and psychological needs.

This tragic formlessness is the result of a contradiction in our social existence. It indicates our failure in the organization of that new equipment with which we must function if we are to maintain our equilibrium in a dynamic world.

Advances in science and technology have created a new dimension. Today, all people of the world are neighbors, and natural resources on a hitherto undreamed of scale are within the potential reach of all. The inherited structure of a smaller, outgrown world, however, stands in the way of the integration of our lives in the terms of the present wider dimension. Totalitarian aggression, as the most destructive aspect of the resistance of the past, sought to direct the present and future toward an obsolete organization, of a necessity employing force in order to accomplish what was diametrically opposed to the principles of growth and development. These destructive forces, on the other hand, inevitably prepare the way for reconstruction. The more unbearable the strains and stresses caused by the contradiction between the potentialities of the present and the outlived forms of the past, the stronger is the compulsion toward equilibrating our life in the contemporary dimension. To achieve a livable life today, then, we must reorient ourselves, and create forms in terms of present historical conditions. Instead of allowing both a further haphazard accumulation of scientific discoveries and a planless technological expansion, it is our task to establish an organic interconnection of the new frontiers of knowledge. Integration, planning, and form are the key words of all progressive efforts today; the goal is a new vital structure-order, a new form on a social plane, in which all present knowledge and technological posessions may function unhindered as a whole.

This new structure-order can be achieved only if man of today becomes truly contemporary and fully able to use his capacities. To be contemporary in a true sense demands a most advanced knowledge of the facts governing life of today. The understanding of vital aspects of our life, however, to most of us is still at the same stage as it was a hundred years ago. In the past, lightning, plague, and famine were believed to be visitations of Providence, but today, through knowledge and understanding, we are able to control them. In like fashion, if we should make social application of scientific knowledge, present obstacles to a contemporary human existence would be eliminated. We must dissipate the belief that war, economic crises, or psychological disintegration is unavoidable and due to blind, inimical forces of nature. The collective efforts of scientists have given us a richer and safer life in the biological and physical realms; we must meet them in

12

socio-economic and psychological realms. Education on an unprecedented scale is imperative if man, who now lives in a wider world, is to be really contemporary.

But this new knowledge can only be the living fibre of integration if man experiences it with the wholeness of his being. Human faculties, however, have been dulled and have disintegrated in a climate of frustration. Experience has tended to become only a stepping-stone to an exploitation of nature and of man. Experiences are isolated pigeon-holes; they display only single aspects of human beings. To function in his fullest scope man must restore the unity of his experiences so that he can register sensory, emotional, and intellectual dimensions of the present in an indivisible whole.

*The **language of vision,** optical communication, is one of the strongest potential means both to reunite man and his knowledge and to re-form man into an integrated being. The visual language is capable of disseminating knowledge more effectively than almost any other vehicle of communication. With it, man can express and relay his experiences in object form. Visual communication is universal and international: it knows no limits of tongue, vocabulary, or grammar, and it can be perceived by the illiterate as well as by the literate. Visual language can convey facts and ideas in a wider and deeper range than almost any other means of communication. It can reinforce the static verbal concept with the sensory vitality of dynamic imagery. It can interpret the new understanding of the physical world and social events because dynamic interrelationships and interpenetration, which are significant of every advanced scientific understanding of today, are intrinsic idioms of the contemporary vehicles of visual communication: photography, motion pictures, and television.*

But the language of vision has a more subtle and, to a certain extent, an even more important contemporary task. To perceive a visual image implies the beholder's participation in a process of organization. The experience of an image is thus a creative act of integration. Its essential characteristic is that by plastic power an experience is formed into an organic whole. Here is a basic discipline of forming, that is, thinking in terms of structure, a discipline of utmost importance in the chaos of our formless world. Plastic arts, the optimum forms of the language of vision, are, therefore, an invaluable educational medium.

Visual language must be readjusted, however, to meet its historical challenge of educating man to a contemporary standard, and of helping him to think in terms of form.

Technological discoveries have extended and reshaped the physical environment. They have changed our visual surroundings partly by actually rebuilding the physical environment, and partly by presenting visual tools that are of assistance to our discernment of those phases of the visible world which were previously too small, too fast, too large, or too slow for us to comprehend. Vision is primarily a device of orientation; a means to meas-

13

ure and organize spatial events. The mastery of nature is intimately con-nected with the mastery of space; this is visual orientation. Each new visual environment demands a reorientation, a new way of measuring. Seeing spatial relationships on a flat land is a different experience from seeing them in a mountainous region, where one form intercepts the other. To orient oneself in walking requires a different spatial measurement than is required in riding in a motor-car or in an aeroplane. To grasp spatial rela-tionships and orient oneself in a metropolis of today, among the intricate dimensions of streets, subways, elevated, and skyscrapers, requires a new way of seeing. Widening horizons, and the new dimensions of the visual environment necessitate new idioms of spatial measurement and communi-cation of space. The visual image of today must come to terms with all this: it must evolve a language of space which is adjusted to the new standards of experience. This new language can and will enable the human sensibility to perceive space-time relationships never recognized before.

Vision is not only orientation in physical spheres but also orientation in human spheres. Man can no more bear chaos in his emotional and intel-lectual life than he can bear it in his biological existence. In each age of human history man was compelled to search for a temporary equilibrium in his conflicts with nature and in his relations with other men, and thus created, through an organization of visual imagery, a symbolic order of his psychological and intellectual experiences. These forms of his creative imagination directed and inspired him toward materializing the potential order inherent in each stage of history. But until today, the symbolic or-ganization of psychological and intellectual conflicts has been limited in its power because it was fastened to a static system of object concepts. Today, the dynamics of social events, and the new vistas of a mobile, physi-cal world, have compelled us to exchange a static iconography for a dynamic one. Visual language thus must absorb the dynamic idioms of the visual imagery to mobilize the creative imagination for positive social action, and direct it toward positive social goals.

Today, creative artists have three tasks to accomplish if the language of vision is to be made a potent factor in reshaping our lives. They must learn and apply the laws of **plastic organization** *needed for the re-establishing of the created image on a healthy basis. They must make terms with con-temporary spatial experiences to learn to utilize the* **visual representation** *of contemporary space-time events. Finally, they must release the reserves of creative imagination and organize them into dynamic idioms, that is, develop a contemporary* **dynamic iconography.**

I. Plastic organization

The created image

We live in the midst of a whirlwind of light qualities. From this whirling confusion we build unified entities, those forms of experience called visual images.

To perceive an image is to participate in a forming process; it is a creative act. From the simplest form of orientation to the most embracing plastic unity of a work of art, there is a common significant basis: the following up of the sensory qualities of the visual field and the organizing of them. Independent of what one "sees," every experiencing of a visual image is a forming; a dynamic process of integration, a "plastic" experience. The word "plastic" therefore is here used to designate the formative quality, the shaping of sensory impressions into unified, organic wholes.●

●*Throughout this discussion and that which follows, it should be understood that all terms used are arbitrary, and are not to be considered as scientifically established. The use of such terms is made necessary by the lack of an adequate terminology in the field of visual experience considered as a creative activity.*

The experience of a plastic image is a form evolved through a process of organization. The plastic image has all the characteristics of a living organism. It exists through forces in interaction which are acting in their respective fields, and are conditioned by these fields. It has an organic, spatial unity; that is, it is a whole the behavior of which is not determined by that of its individual components, but where the parts are themselves determined by the intrinsic nature of the whole. It is, therefore, an enclosed system that reaches its dynamic unity by various levels of integration; by balance, rhythm and harmony.

The experiencing of every image is the result of an interaction between external physical forces and internal forces of the individual as he assimilates, orders, and molds external forces to his own measure. The external forces are light-agents bombarding the eye and producing changes on the retina. The internal forces constitute the dynamic tendency of the individual to restore balance after each disturbance from the outside, and thus to keep his system in relative stability.

Every force acts in a medium, exists in a field. Any process induced by forces makes sense only with reference to the surroundings, as an interaction between the force and the medium in which it acts. One walks against the resistance of the earth, the spatial extension of the objective world. One flies, buoyed up by the resistance of the air. The frame of reference or field in which one force acts conditions the range and path of the action induced. The weight and shape of a material as well as the nature of the resisting medium will define the manifestations of the force of gravity. A pebble dropped through air behaves differently from one dropped into water, snow, mercury, or mud.

Optical forces and the physiological and psychological responses which they induce also are meaningful only in their respective fields. The external optical forces which provide the physical bases of the experience which we call the plastic image, and the internal forces—the dynamic tendency to integrate the impacts of the environment—act within their respective frames of reference. It must be borne in mind, however, that it is the nervous system which organizes impacts from the outside. Therefore, the distinction between external and internal frames of reference is, in a sense, artificial and is used only for convenience, since in every experience the external frame of reference is transformed into a part of the internal one.

External forces

The plastic image as a dynamic experience begins with the light-energy flowing through the spectator's eye to his nervous system. For example, this light-energy is articulated on a picture-surface in different extensions by different pigments. The nature of the pigments provides the basis for sensations of light and color; that is, brightness, hue and saturation. The geometrical demarcation of these qualities provide the physical basis for perception of areas and their shapes. Altogether, these factors constitute the vocabulary of the language of vision, and are acting as the optical forces of attraction.

16

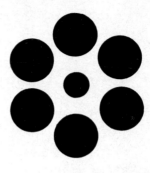

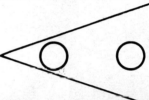

Visual illusion of size and direction

The visual field, the retinal field

The forces of visual attraction—a point, a line, an area—exist in an optical background and act on the optical field. This optical field is projected on the retinal surface of the eyes as an inseparable background for the distinct visual units. One can not therefore perceive visual units as isolated entities, but relationships. "As so called optical illusions show, we do not see individual fractions of a thing; instead, the mode of appearance of each part depends not only upon the stimulation arising at that point but upon the conditions prevailing at other points as well."•

Color and value depend always upon the immediate surrounding surfaces. A brightness value can be amplified or blotted out by the other values. A color can be intensified or neutralized in the same way.

The same is true of texture-qualities. Sizes and shapes likewise are perceived only in polar unity with a background and their specific optical quality is due to their respective frames of reference. A slightly irregular shape appears strongly irregular in a frame of reference of geometrically perfect squares, but the same shape appears perfectly regular in reference to extremely irregular units. Generally speaking, all the optical units on a picture-surface derive their qualities in relationship to their respective backgrounds, ranging from the immediate surrounding surface to the optical field as a whole.

•*W. Kohler, Physikal Gestalten 1920*

Visual illusion of values

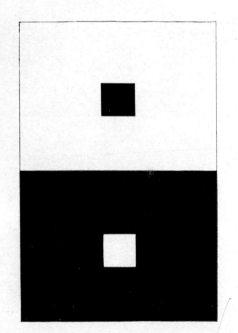

There can be, therefore, neither an absolute quality of color, brightness, saturation, nor absolute measure of size, length and shape on the optical field, because each visual unit gains its unique mode of appearance in a dynamic interrelationship with its optical environment. Here is an important point. The range of hue, value, saturation, and the scale of geometrical measure is incomparably narrower on the picture surface than in one's visible surroundings and only by a creative use of the relativity of optical differences can one create an optical image on the surface that stands up to the vitality of the visible world.

"The sky in a landscape may be thousands of times brighter than a deep shadow or a hole in the ground. A cumulus cloud in the sky may be hundred thousands brighter than the deepest shadow. However, the artist must represent a landscape by means of a palette whose white is only about thirty times brighter than the black."●

●*M. Luckiesh, Visual illusions.*

The three-dimensional field

Looking at a landscape, at people on the street, or at any single object, as the visual field has no definite boundaries, one can only make a spatial interpretation of the things he sees—their location, extension—based upon his own spatial position. He judges the position, direction and interval of things seen by relating them to himself. He measures and organizes up, down, left, right, advance, and recession in a single physical system of which his body is the center and identified with the main directions in space. The ego-centered horizontal and vertical axis is the latent background, and optical differences are interpreted against this background. If the spectator moves his head, eye, or body—changing his position and consequently changing the retinal field from the natural vertical position,—he at once transfers to the objects nearest him the original role of the human body and the main directions of space remain valid.

The picture field

The visual field of a picture image is less diffused. It is limited to the boundaries of a picture-plane, and to the two dimensions of this surface.

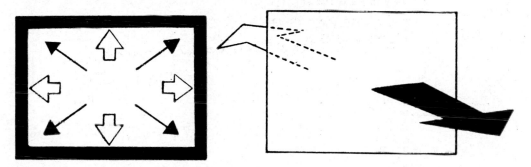

The frame of reference shifts from the more general spatial direction of the spectator to the new background of picture field—to the four borders and the two dimensions. An entirely new frame of reference is created, a world with new laws formed out of the new relations.

The four borders of the picture-plane generally assume the main directions of space, and each distinct optical unit on the surface receives its spatial evaluation, its position, direction, and interval because of its relationship to the margins considered as the horizontal and vertical axes of the newly created world. The two-dimensional picture plane assumes the center of the spatial field and every optical unit appears to advance or recede from it. A point, a line, or a shape on the picture-surface is seen as possessing spatial qualities. If one places a point or a line in one or another position on the surface, the position of the respective optical units in reference to the picture margin will relate different spatial meanings as a dynamic form of movement. The elements appear to be moving left, right, up, down, and to be receding or advancing, depending upon their respective position in the picture-plane. The optical units create an interpretation of the surface as a spatial world; they have strength and direction, they become spatial forces.

The spatial forces

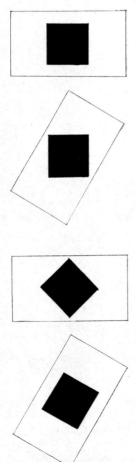

A stone, a tree, or a fish has its own particular type of existence. The stone is static with the latent perpendicular movement of its weight. The tree can expand in any direction but cannot change its position. The fish can move and take any position. Each behaves according to its specific nature. Similarly, any visible unit placed on a picture-plane germinates a life of its own.

Positions, directions and differences in size, shape, brightness, color and texture are measured and assimilated by the eye. The eye lends the character of its neuro-muscular experience to its source. Since each shape, color, value, texture, direction, and position produces a different quality of experience, there must arise an inherent contradiction from their being on the same flat surface. This contradiction can be resolved only as they have the appearance of movement in the picture-plane. These virtual movements of optical qualities will mould and form the picture space, thus acting as spatial forces. Only incidentally does the spatial quality derive from the fact that optical signs resemble objects known empirically. One experiences space when looking at an articulated two-dimensional surface mainly because one unconsciously attempts to organize and perceive the different sensations induced by the optical qualities and measures as a whole, and in so doing is forced, by the various qualities in their relationships to each other and to the picture-surface, to impute spatial meaning to these relationships.

In the diagram taken from Kopferman, the black squares in a rectangular outline which indicates the boundaries of the picture-plane demonstrate the modifications of the same shape under various conditions. Wherever the small square can be brought into accordance with the main direction of space it is seen as a square, partly because it is parallel with the borders of the picture-plane, and partly because it is actually in a horizontal-vertical position in regard to the next frame of reference—the page. It is thus dependent upon the ground on which it appears. If the ground has a definite correspondence to the horizontal-vertical axis, however, the square figure in a diagonal position not only loses its stability but undergoes a modification. It is seen, not as a square, but as a diamond. A study of the diagram makes it obvious that the relationship of the unit to the picture-border generates its spatial expression. In one case it appears static and suspended; in another, static but with strong resistance—almost with a quality of solidity; in a third case, it changes shape and loses its concreteness; finally, it suggests a potential movement and fluctuates between the square and the diamond shape.

Whether we wish it or not, any optical differentiation of a picture surface generates a sense of space. A typographical design, scribbling on paper, color spots on a canvas, a photograph, a simple haphazard manipulation of light or a painting with an explosive emotional message—all these are spatial expressions by virtue of the process through which the eye organizes their visible differences into a whole.

Picasso. *Crying Woman 1936*

Reproduction Courtesy
The Art Institute of Chicago

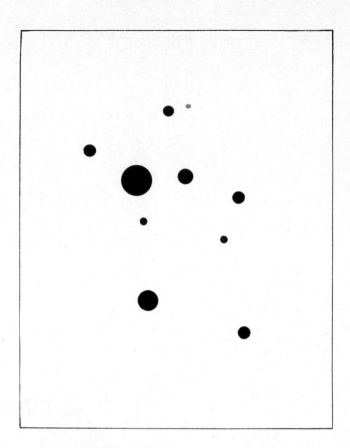

Kandinsky. *9 Points In Ascendance*

Malevich. *Sensation of Flight 1914-15*

El Lissitzky. *Illustration 1923*

Before one begins to use the visual language for the communication of a concrete message, he should learn the greatest possible variety of spatial sensations inherent in the relationships of the forces acting on the picture-surface. The storing up of such varied experience is the most important part of the training for visual expression. What is called technical education, the mastery of a particular skill or a particular habit of visual representation, should be put off as long as one learns the objective basis of the language of vision. A playful manipulation of each element: points, shapes, lines—varying them in position, in color, in value, and in texture—is the shortest way to an understanding of their interrelationships. Just as the letters of the alphabet can be put together in innumerable ways to form words which convey meanings, so the optical measures and qualities can be brought together in innumerable ways, and each particular relationship generates a different sensation of space. The variations to be achieved are endless. For while the elementary signs of the English language are only twenty-six, the number of elementary forces with which the machinery of sight is provided is prodigious.

A color spot generates different experiences of space depending upon whether it is placed in the middle of the picture-plane, to the left or right, or at the top or bottom. Each unique interrelationship yields a unique spatial feeling. The introduction of more than one spot increases the sensation of space. The spots move away from or toward each other, receding or advancing, and seem to have weight or a centripetal or centrifugal direction. A still more vital spatial event is created when these surface areas are articulated in size, color. Straight and curvular lines in a horizontal, vertical, or diagonal relationship to the picture-margin force the eye to orient and explore the surface in a different way and originate another variety of spatial sensation. An even richer spatial expression can be created by manipulating various shapes on the picture-surface. Their value, color, texture, and relative position induce spatial experiences of further intensity and variety.

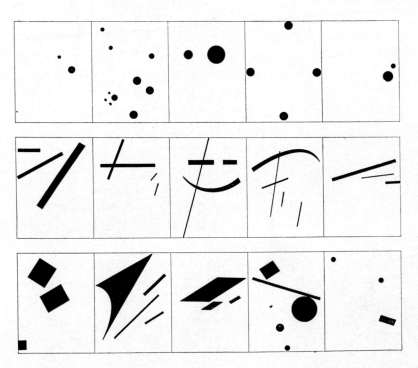

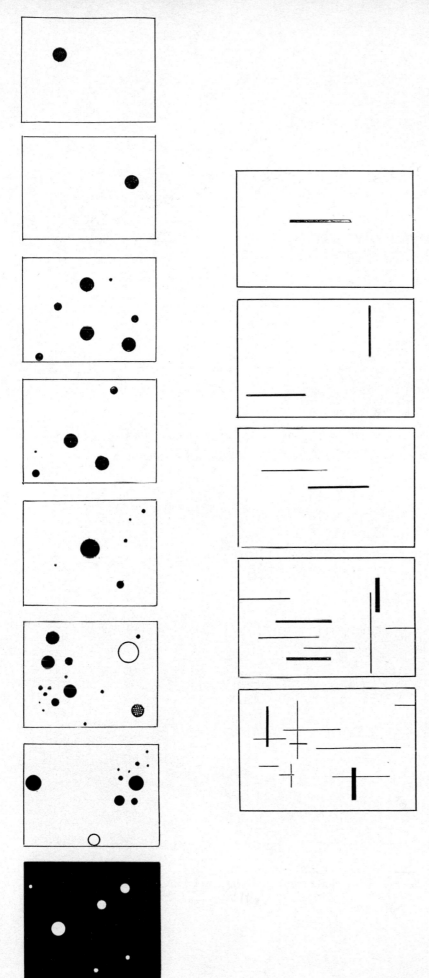

Adeline Cross. *Study of the advancing and receding space qualities of tone values.*
Work done for the author's course in Visual Fundamentals. School of Design in Chicago.

Study of the advancing and receding qualities of colors

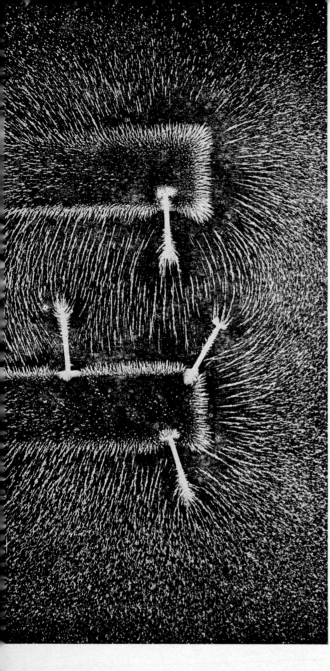

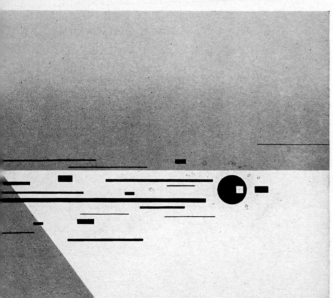

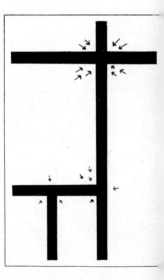

Magnetic field

H. L. Carpenter.
The attraction and repulsion of the space forces.
Work done for the author's course in Visual Fundamentals. School of Design in Chicago

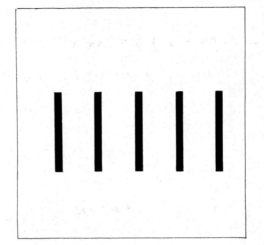 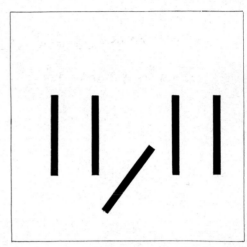

Fields of spatial forces

A human being is more than his own body; he implies those actions which reach out and transform his environment. A magnetized bar of steel is more than its own mass; its electrical field belongs to it just as much as do its substance, its shape and its weight. The picture-surface becomes a vital spatial world, not only in the sense that the spatial forces are acting on it—moving, falling and circulating —but also in the sense that between these movements the field itself is charged with action. The actual visual elements are only the focal points of this field; they are the concentrated energy. Color, value, texture, point, line and area radiate different amounts of energy, and thus each element or quality can encompass a different radius of the picture-surface. These fields extend into every dimension and each field has its own unique form.

The fields of the forces may be interrupted, or they may impinge upon each other. A field intercepting another field, attracts or repels it; reinforces it or interferes with it. This interaction of one field with another causes strains and stresses. When two lines cross, for example, the fields of forces fight and the spatial energies are concentrated in the reflecting angle.

Internal forces

Every living organism—be it a plant, an animal, a human being, or a social structure—is a relatively constant form. As the wheels of a bicycle stand erect only through perpetual movement, so the organism keeps its form through constant motion. A plant, for example, by the perpetual process of metabolism, draws upon sunlight, water, soil, retaining only what it needs to keep its organism relatively stable. To maintain the same constant structure, every living organism must achieve a dynamic unity. The plastic image is no exception. Only by dynamic order can it become a living form of human experience. "The eye especially demands completeness," says Goethe. Internal forces are acting to restore balance after each disturbance from the outside.

Changes produced by light on the retina are balanced by physiological reactions. When light-energy induces physiological disturbances in the retina, using up certain chemical substances, etc., the organism in general and the retina in particular restore the used-up substances. When certain muscular actions enforced by the distribution of light on the visual field induce fatigue, the organism answers with a complementary movement, bringing into action fresh neuro-muscular units. As any worker changes, from time to time, the rhythm of his work, the eye, or rather the neuromuscular apparatus, tends to find the same relief from fatigue, an experience of balance. Each impact upon the eye from outside is counteracted by a reciprocal movement from inside. If the eye is hit by a sudden intensive light beam, it is automatically closed. But the eye has also more positive and subtle reactions to light stimulation. If red light rays beat upon it over a prolonged period of time, it reacts, when turned away from the red surface, by seeing a green after-image immediately. The biological organism acts to restore the sensitivity of the surface which was kept in action by giving it full rest.

30

The dynamic tendency toward balance is not restricted to a biological level. Sight is more than pure sensation, for light rays reaching the eye have no intrinsic order as such. They are only a haphazard, chaotic panorama of mobile, independent light-happenings. As soon as they reach the retina, the mind organizes and molds them into meaningful spatial units. We cannot bear chaos—the disturbance of equilibrium in the field of experience. Consequently, we must immediately form light-impacts into shapes and figures. Exposed to a visual field that in its light-quality is to the slightest degree heterogeneous, one organizes that field at once into two opposing elements; into a figure against a background. One speaks of white with inevitable implied reference to black, grey, or other colors. To convey the meaning of "yes," one implies a latent understanding of "no." A unified whole is thus created. Every image is based upon this dynamic dualism, the unity of opposites. Certain impulses are tied together in a stable visual whole, while other impulses are left in their unorganized fluid state and serve only as a background and are perceived as intervals. This organization of figures and backgrounds is repeated progressively until the whole visual field is perceived as a formed, ordered unity—the plastic image.

Fluctuation of the figure and background.

Mi Yujen. *Landscape.*
The Cleveland Museum of Art

In every clear concept of the nature of vision and in every healthy approach to the spatial world, this dynamic unity of figure and background has been clearly understood. Lao Tse showed such grasp when he said: "A vessel is useful only through its emptiness. It is the space opened in a wall that serves as a window. Thus it is the nonexistent in things which makes them serviceable." Eastern visual culture has a deep understanding of the role of the empty space in the image. Chinese and Japanese painters have the admirable courage to leave empty large paths of their picture-surface so that the surface is divided into unequal intervals which, through their spacing, force the eye of the spectator to movements of varying velocity in following up relationships, and thus create the unity by the greatest possible variation of surface. Chinese and Japanese calligraphy also has a sound respect for the white interval. Characters are written in imaginary squares, the blank areas of which are given as much consideration as the graphic units, the strokes. Written or printed communication is living or dead depending upon the organization of its blank spaces. A single character gains clarity and meaning by orderly relationship of the space background which surrounds it. The greater the variety and distinction among respective background units, the clearer becomes the comprehension of a character as an individual expression or sign.

The meaning of space interval is coming to be understood also in architecture. For a time the idea of integration of spatial structures, organic form, in which figure and background are considered in a unity of mutual interdependence, was lost in the wild haste of technological progress. Every new invention, every new scientific discovery, every new product, was considered without reference to its implications for human life. But we are witnessing now a reorientation toward a more integrated life achieved through progressive recognition of the interconnection of figure and background. Contemporary architects are moving away from one-sided emphasis on the façade of a building, and the best examples of contemporary architecture show a perfect integration of the actual building, the active "envelope," the divisions created by the materials, and the living spaces between these materials. Light screens, curtains, glass walls are employed to amplify this integration optically and to create a living, flowing space articulated within and without: a single living unity.

The same trend is prevailing in science. Says Erwin Schrodinger:

"We are no longer afraid of broad empty spaces in our furniture or on our walls. We haven't what the German call 'platz angst'—the fear of the empty spaces—any more. . . . Now, there is something similar in our science. . . . We want no ornamental accessories. Just as we are no longer afraid of bare surfaces on our furniture and dwelling rooms, so in our scientific picture of the external world we do not try to fill out the empty spaces."•

•*Erwin Schrodinger, Physical Science and the Temper of the Age.*

Calligraphy in Ts'Ao (running cursive) Style by Su Tung-P'o.

From a rubbing in the Berthold Laufer Collection, Field Museum of Natural History, Chicago. Courtesy of Miss Lucy Driscoll

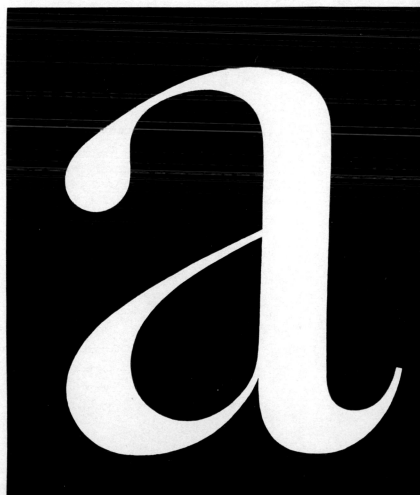

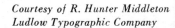
Courtesy of R. Hunter Middleton Ludlow Typographic Company

The fields of the internal forces

The dynamic tendency to integrate optical impacts into a balanced, unified whole acts within the field of the physiological and psychological make-up of man. The forces driving toward the restoration of equilibrium in the human organism are nervous forces, and the nervous system, like the picture plane, is limited. Just as limitations of the picture-surface serve as the necessary frame of reference in the transformation of optical impacts into spatial forces, so the characteristics of the physiological and psychological mechanisms serve as the conditioning factors in experiencing forces of integration, that is, transforming spatial forces into plastic forces.

The physiological field

The balance in the physiological dimensions is conditioned by the limitations of the eye.

"For the eye has every possible defect that can be found in an optical instrument, and even some which are peculiar to itself; but they are all so counteracted, that the inexactness of the image which results from their presence very little exceeds, under ordinary conditions of illumination, the limits which are set to the delicacy of sensation by the dimensions of the retinal cones. But as soon as we make our observation under somewhat changed conditions, we become aware of the chromatic aberration, the astigmatism, the blind spot, the venous shadows, the imperfect transparency of the media, and all the other defects of which we have spoken."●

The eye is so constructed that it can focus images upon only a very small area of the retinal field. To obtain sufficient focused data, it must rotate in the area of things to be perceived. This limitation is the basis of numerous delicate muscle movements which are registered as sensations and interpreted as spatial signs. The eye, focusing red light from an infinite distance upon the retina, will, at the same time, focus violet rays from a distance of two feet. If different color-surfaces are the same distance from the eyes, as on a two-dimensional picture-plane, a muscular adjustment is required to bring the different rays successively into focus. These adjustments are registered as different sensations, and, associating their qualities with respective colors, create spatial sensations.

●*H. W. Helmholtz, Physiological Optics*

34

Color balance

Like every other part of the human body, the eye has a natural limit of working capacity. After a certain performance it becomes fatigued. But as it was pointed out previously, the physiological forces are driving for an equilibrium to keep the systems essentially constant. "Every decided color does a certain violence to the eye, and forces the organ to opposition," said Goethe. After each fatigue of the ocular apparatus, after each destruction of certain photochemical substances on the retina, making it insensitive to one or another color, there is a dynamic tendency to gain back the original order, the full sensitivity, a physiological balance.

"If we look steadily at some brightly colored object for a few seconds and then look away at an illuminated surface, preferably white, we see a patch of a different color, which floats before our eyes and moves as we turn them. The explanation is that the receivers on the retina are not equally fatigued. If we have been looking at red, the red receiver is more fatigued than the other so that when white light is thrown into the eye, the two other receivers are more fully stimulated and a bluish green appears."[•]

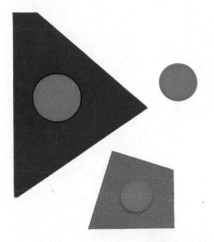

"If we admit light from a cloudy sky through a narrow opening into a dark room, so that it falls sideways on a horizontal sheet of white paper, while candle-light falls on it from the other side, and if we then hold a pencil vertically upon the paper, it will of course throw two shadows: the one made by the daylight will be orange, and looks so; the other made by the candle-light is really white, but appears blue by contrast. The blue and the orange of the two shadows are both colours which we call white, when we see them by daylight and candle-light respectively. Seen together, they appear as two very different and tolerably saturated colours, yet we do not hesitate a moment in recognizing white paper by candle-light as white, and very different from orange."[• •]

This "after image," colored shadows, and various other visual phenomena, border contrast and simultaneous contrast, point toward the most significant characteristics of color surfaces as plastic forces. Through a dynamic interaction of the surfaces on the picture-plane, the colors tend toward a balanced relationship in the terms of a full retinal sensitivity. Each hue induces simultaneously or in succession its respective complementary part, returning to its origin, that, is the white light. Roughly speaking, a red surface will induce a blue green, a certain blue violet will create a complementary yellow, orange brings out turquoise blue. Complementary color harmony—the most universally accepted law of plastic balance—has its foundation here. Although there are minor disparities in the interpretation of what opposite hues are, color automatism in children's paintings, color expressions of almost all cultures, scientific research of the great thinkers—Leonardo, Goethe, Schopenhauer, Chevreul, Ostwald—testify the universal validity of color harmony as a conformity to the law of the human organism, an equilibrium in visual experience.

Adjacent color surfaces modify each other in hue and brightness.

[•] *H. Helmholtz, Recent Progress of the Theory of Vision, 1868*
[• •] *Sir W. Bragg, The Universe of Light*

Spatial tension; dynamic equilibrium

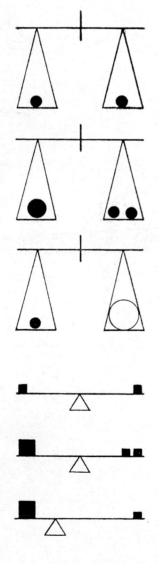

A two-dimensional surface without any articulation is a dead experience. The basis of every living process is an inner contradiction. The living-quality of an image is generated by the tension between the spatial forces; that is, by the struggle between the attraction and repulsion of the fields of these forces.

The experience of space, as we have already seen, is based upon the virtual movement of the different optical units from the picture-plane. These movements can be perceived only if the frame of reference, the two-dimensional picture-plane, is evident; one cannot see moving things without a background. Considered singly, each optical force automatically interrupts the two-dimensional quality of the picture-surface and completes its virtual movement by inducing its own field. It becomes impossible, therefore, to perceive the dynamic factor of this movement. Here is an important point. Just as any force can be manifested only through resistance to an opposite force, so spatial forces may be perceived only as they meet opposing spatial forces. A random placing of spatial forces, point, line, area, will open the picture-plane, but because these forces are so haphazardly arranged, they will not reach a balanced constellation in which they are equal in strength and opposite in direction. The picture surface is made hollow; the two-dimensional background, the frame of reference in which the spatial movements can be measured, is missing. The spatial vitality cannot reach full maturity.

If the forces and their induced fields are of equal optical quality and spatial strength, a balance will be reached, but it will be without tension, static and lifeless. If, however, one knows how to estimate the forces and their energy-field, he will be able to use such opposing fields so that each will balance the other on the picture-plane. A line or shape in a certain color and position will have a field opened and advancing toward the spectator; another unit will create a field in a receding direction; another will activate a field tending upward on the surface; and yet another, down. These movements may be different in terms of their optical measures and qualities—that is, opposite in direction, weight, intensity—but, if they are equal in strength in terms of their spatial fields, a dynamic equilibrium will be reached on the picture surface.

If one sees on scales a pound of iron balancing a pound of feathers, one becomes involved in the experience because of the apparent optical contradiction in logic. One is forced to think about the nature of the opposing materials and grasp their further relationships. The sight of an adult balanced by a small child on a see-saw, because of their different distances from the center of gravity, induces a similar experience. This dynamic balancing may also be simply illustrated by crushing a piece of paper in the hand. Lying flat, that paper is inert, dead. As it is compressed, it acquires a kinetic quality. Hand and paper each exert strong fields of force which oppose each other but which are nevertheless in balance.

36

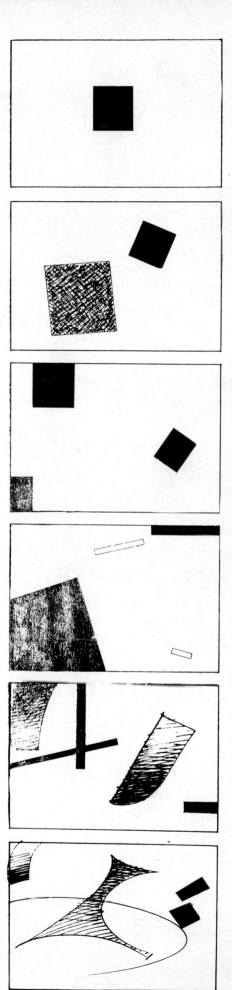

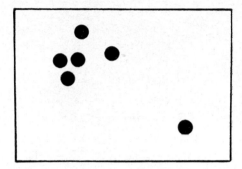

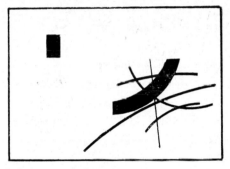

The point of the retina on the optical axis of the eye provides visual acuteness. The geometrical center of the picture field is customarily identified with the optical axis and is assumed as the center of gravity of all forces acting on the picture surface.

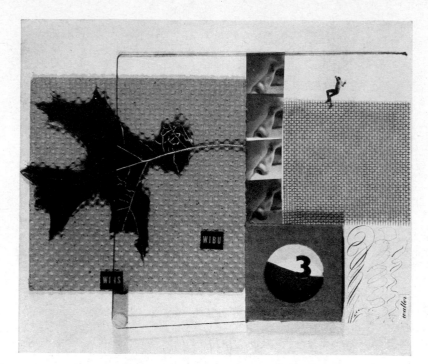

Harold Walter. *Collage 1939*

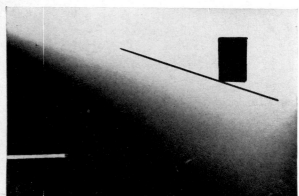

Kasimir Malevich. *Suprematist Composition* 👉

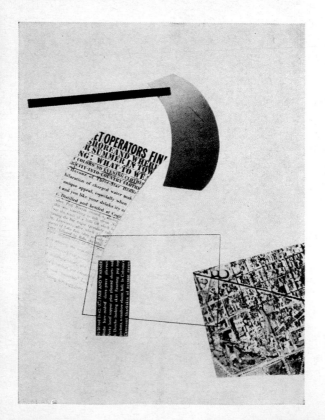

Ruth Robbins. *Study of dynamic equilibrium in texture values.*
Work done for the author's course in Visual Fundamentals.
School of Design in Chicago.

Jean Helion. *Linoleum Cut 1932*

40

El Lissitzky. *Proun 1923*

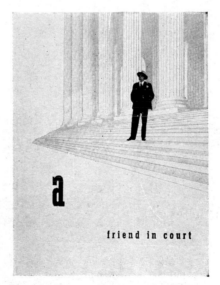

Lester Beall. *Advertising Design*

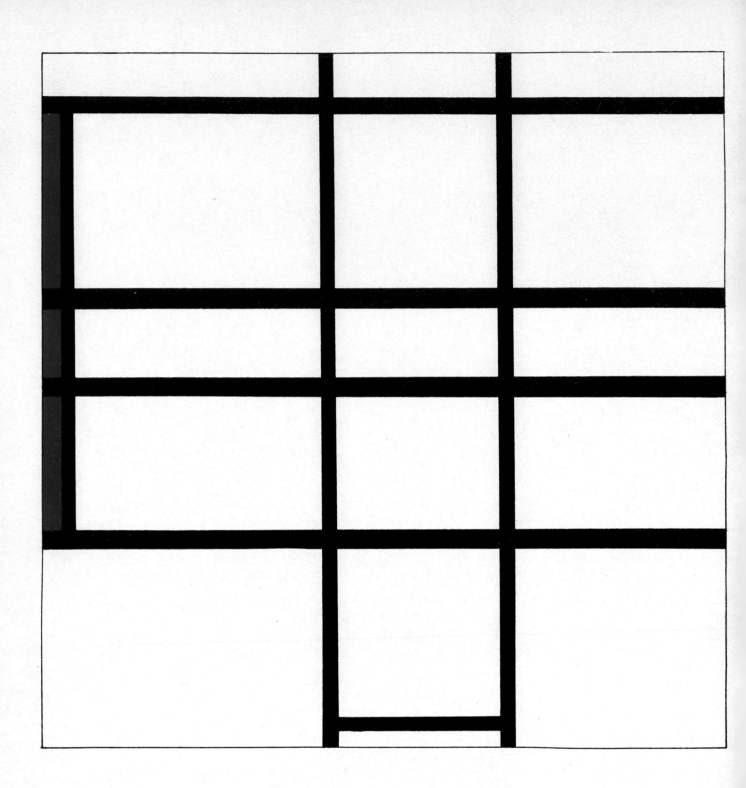

Piet Mondrian. *Composition with Red 1936*
Courtesy of The Philadelphia Museum of Art, A. E. Gallatin Collection

Jan Tschichold:

Typographische Gestaltung

Benno Schwabe & Co . Basel 1935

The psychological field

Subjective forces tending toward balance are manifested in the emotional and intellectual faculties as well as on the physiological level. The plastic image is an organism that reaches out to the dimensions of understanding beyond the sensory radius. The fascination of a sunset or a sunrise, the irresistible interest aroused by the ever-changing shapes and colors of flames, or the rhythmical patterns and reflections of waves on the water, have a revealing meaning. We never tire of these optical transformations which, in spite of all variations, retain their unity. We follow the innumerable mutations without any feeling of compulsion. The significant aspect of such experiences is that they mobilize wider responses, thoughts, and feelings not directly connected with the actual seen image. As a little boy is able to move a large church-bell by the rhythmical addition of one pull to another, the rhythmical order of flames or waves can induce larger and larger, wider and wider, dimensions of experience. From the perception of sensory patterns, one moves to corresponding structures in emotional and intellectual realms. The experience becomes complete. To reach balance in this wider dimension, the dynamic bases, the space-time span of the plastic experience must be secured.

The dynamic tendency to organize the optical forces into a unified whole acts within the psychological field against a background of readiness to perceive—a field of attention. Attention, however, suffers from two limitations: first, its limitation in the number of optical units it can encompass; and second, its limited duration in time of focus on one optical situation. And just as the limitations of the two-dimensional picture field serve as a necessary frame of reference to the virtual locations of the optical units, so the limitations of the psychological field serve as the necessary condition to the laws of plastic organization.

The space span of plastic organization

To be seen in a purely sensory way, an optical unit must fall on the small retinal region of clear vision; to be seen in terms of perceptual grasp, the image must fall within the limited field of the attentive act. "The process of visual organization might be considered as a figure against the background of the field of consciousness. In the blurred general field an area of clearness and intensity is formed—the field of attention." Within this field of attention one can see clearly, and at one time, only a limited number of visual units. The extent of this vividness and clearness is determined by the energy of the attentive act. This attentive energy is sufficient for grasping and relating only a limited number of optical units. In fact, only five or six optically distinct elements can be seen together clearly in their individual characteristics and relationships.

44

Confronted with a complex optical field, one will reduce it to basic inter-relationships. Just as in nature there is a tendency to find the most economic surface unity in every formation, so in the visual organization there is a tendency to find the most economic spatial unity in the ordering of optical differences. Facing the turmoil of optical impacts, one's first reaction is to form in the shortest time interval the greatest possible spatial span.

Certain optical characteristics tend to be seen together as a spatial configuration. As we look at a greatly-enlarged half-tone screen, what we actually see are different sizes of black dots and different white intervals. But instantly we organize and group these visible differences. Some units of black dots are seen in one form; some in another. Some elements are seen together because they are close to each other; others are bound together because they are similar in size, direction, shape. Only after this instantaneous organization is achieved can one see the resemblance of the picture to a human eye.

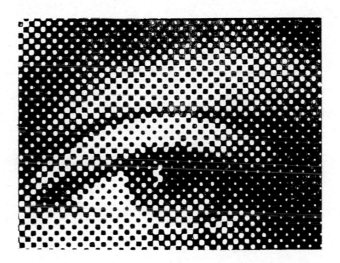

This organization of optical belonging is more basic than the recognition of the objects themselves. The numerous optical devices which nature employs in the animal world to conceal animals from their enemies reveal the workings of this law of visual organization. A snake camouflaged by nature is no longer a snake. It is an aggregation of small units of color-shape. Because kinship of elementary visual qualities is more fundamental to image building than the relations of empirical experience, the patterns on its body are more easily seen together with corresponding patterns in its background than is its form—knowledge of which is acquired in one's other experience. The snake disappears into its background.

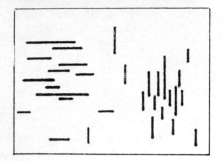

Nearness

Proximity is the simplest condition of organization. We hear words in verbal coherency, primarily because of the temporal proximity of their sound elements. We read words as segregated wholes because their letters are closer to one another than are the last and the first letter of two words. We form the stars of the firmament into a variety of patterns, primarily because of their relative nearness to one another. Generally speaking, the relatively closest distance between sensory units offers the least resistance to their inter-connection, and thus makes possible the beginning of crystallization into a stable form. In the field of visual experience also the proximity of optical units is the simplest condition for a crystallization of unified visual "wholes." We articulate a painting, a typographical design, first of all by the law of proximity. Optical units close to each other on a picture-plane tend to be seen together and, consequently, one can stabilize them in coherent figures.

An illustration taken from K. Koffka can elucidate the law of proximity. Two parallel lines are perceived as one unit if they are close enough together. Because the space between them is enclosed, it appears separated from the surrounding space. If one adds two more parallels outside of the first two, the figure that was made by the interval between them loses its quality as a coherent whole, and serves only as a background for the two new units.

spatial organisation is the vital
factor in an optical message

sp atialor gani sationist hevital
fa ctorin an optical message

spatial organisation is the vital
fa ctorin   an optical message

Analysis of the visual tension created by opposing organizational directions.

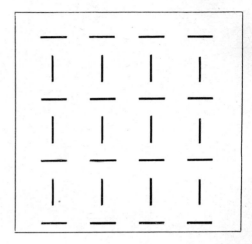

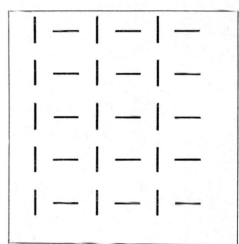

Detail of
Piet Mondrian's Composition 1915.

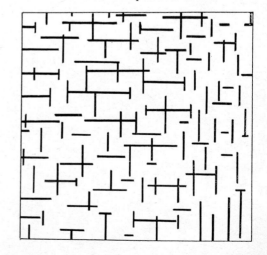

Similarity or equality

Proximity however can yield to other factors of organization. We also tie elements into stable relationships if they have common qualities. Equal sizes, similar shapes, directions, corresponding colors, values, textures also produce the dynamic tendency to be seen together. Proximity and similarity, as factors in the creation of spatial structure, must be considered together. For units formed by proximity can be broken up through the similarity of their elements with other elements at a distance, and units formed by similarity can be broken up by extreme proximity of outside elements. This competition is important to the plastic organism, for opposite direction of organizations can bring a vital tension into the plastic experience. Considering them together, "similarity groups" seem to be more unified than "proximity groups."

Theo Van Doesburg. *Painting*
Courtesy of The Museum of Modern Art

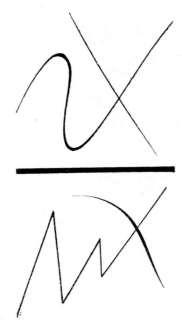

R. J. Wolff. *Painting 1941*

_ *Continuance*

Every linear unit has kinetic inertia. It tends to be continued in the same direction and with the same movement. A straight line tends to be seen in its continuation as a straight line; a curvular line as a curvular line; a wavy line with continuing repetition of its original rhythm. Such linear continuation helps to form the image by creating groups of a simple order. It is a most potent device in binding together heterogeneous elements and thus reducing the picture-image to the number of units which can be fully comprehended in one attentive act.

The law of continuance is also valid for the graduation or progression of hue, value and chroma. The eye moves along a direction of hue or value gradation similar to the way it moves along a line.

49

L. Moholy Nagy. *Stairway 1936*

L. Moholy Nagy. *Photogram 1941*

Closure

Forces of organization driving toward spatial order, toward stability, tend to shape optical units into closed compact wholes. Confronted with a complex optical situation, the beholder searches for the form with the most stable unity, or with the least disturbed relationships to the environment. Goethe observed that the after-image of a sharp square gradually becomes rounded into a circular shape. Just as a drop of water tends to adapt its shape to the most economical surface, so an optical unit tends to form the most economical closure, segregating itself as completely as possible from its surroundings. A closed area appears more formed, more stable, than one which is open and without boundaries. A psychological filling-out of the intervals between the units occurs, and one constructs latent connections. This factor of closure may act on the flat dimension, generating from open linear units the experience of a closed shape, but it may also unify further dimensions. Certain latent inter-connections of points, lines, shapes, colors, and values are closed psychologically into bi-dimensional or tri-dimensional wholes. The factor of closure can be more significant than either nearness or similarity.

Due to the laws of visual organization, no visual unit can exist in itself on the picture-plane. Each unit leads beyond itself and implies a larger whole. Thus units not only live on the picture-plane; they also grow. They merge into wholes with a common function. Three musical tones have each its particular wave length, its individual tonal quality; but when the three are sounded together their individual characteristics retreat and something entirely new appears—the chord. Similarly, the optical units organized into spatial configurations become more than the sum total of their component parts. These larger wholes form with other groups a still farther-reaching unit, and this process continues until all possible relationships are exhausted; that is, until the limit of attention is reached. This law of organization implies, then, that the numerical increase of elements does not necessarily lead to a loss of order of the picture whole. A uniform picture surface is flat. A gradual increase of the elements upon that surface shows clearly that, in each addition to the number or quality of units, a spatial unity can be maintained. Reaching the numeric limit of organization, previously separate units, in a kind of revolutionary leap, form a common figure—and thus a new condition for the organization of a more embracing whole. The number of units can be increased in so far as they do not interfere, forming further units. But when this point of saturation is reached, there is no further opportunity for plastic organization. A uniformity of surface is produced on a new level.

The life-span of the plastic image

The limitations of our nervous system define not only the number and extension of the individual optical units which can be perceived as a whole, that is, the space-span, but also the life-span of the visual experience. One cannot look at a static relationship long without losing interest any more than one can survive for long in a sealed room where the supply of oxygen is soon exhausted. The image as a living experience cannot long exist in a frozen structure. For the image to remain a living organism, relationships within it must be constantly changing. The eye and the mind must be fed with changing visual relationships. Only this changing variety can provide the stimulation necessary for holding attention upon the picture surface. Change implies motion. The plastic image must also be articulated, therefore, in the time dimension. The ultimate aim of plastic organization is a structure of movement that dictates the direction and the progression toward ever new spatial relationships until the experience achieves its fullest spatial saturation. As new relationships progressively unfold, the spatial integration of the image gains momentum until it finds final clarification in the plastic image as a whole. Such movement is defined and conditioned by physiological and psychological limitations. As the movement is basically an eye movement, understanding of the conditioning role of the neuromuscular structure is of great importance. Nevertheless, the direction of interest is what binds one unit to another. The ultimate range of a created image is defined by the available energies of attention.

Organization of optical sequence. Rhythm

Vision is the work process of the eye. Organizing the image means measuring and relating visible differences—hue, value, saturation, texture, position, shape, direction, interval, size—by the neuromuscular action of the eye. Unbroken activity burns out nervous energies. The eye as it works needs both action and repose. The balance of the complementary components must be recognized. Without it, the expenditure of energy, wrongly measured, leads to fatigue. With the correct effort, with a recognized metre, work is done economically and with greater endurance. Wood-chopping, hammering, swimming, rowing, walking, running, dancing are familiar activities in which the metre makes work easier and at the same time endows it with the feeling of pleasure. The proportion of action and repose—that is, the rhythm—depends upon the nature of the work. The orderly repetition or regular alternation of optical similarities or equalities dictates the rhythm of the plastic organization. In recognizing such order one learns when the next eye action is due and what particular neuromuscular adjustment will be necessary to grasp the next unit. To conserve the attentive energies of vision, therefore, the picture surface must have a temporal structure of organization—it must be rhythmically articulated in a way that corresponds, for the eye, to the rhythm of any work process.

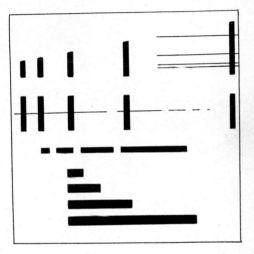

But the significance of rhythm goes far beyond the crude material of pleasure in energy saving. Rhythm cannot be grasped as one isolated visual sensation. Its very meaning lies in the fact that it is an order of a greater temporal whole. The sparing of mental energies in judging the necessary physiological measures makes sense only in reference to the whole building process of the image.

Once a metre of accent and pause is recognized, a dynamic unity is formed, a time-binding order. Up and down, left and right, straight and curved, light and dark, small and large, short and long, condensation and rarefaction, and other optical characteristics are tied by a common measure into an organic succession which braces the attention in a continuous flow until all relationships are evolved into a unity. Plotinus phrased this truth correctly long ago. He wrote:

"What is it, that impresses you when you look at something, attracts you, captivates you and fills you with joy? We are all agreed, I may say, that it is the inter-relation of parts toward one another and towards the whole, with the added element of beauty in colour, which constitutes beauty as perceived by the eye, in other words, that beauty in visible things as in everything else consists of symmetry and proportion."

53

1. *Star of Phytagoras*
2. *The Divine Proportion*
3. *Star of Phytagoras in*

   Regular Pentagram

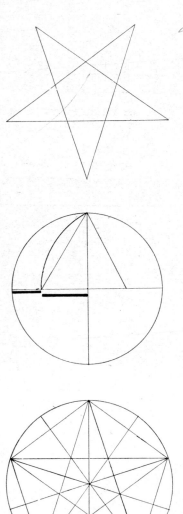

Rhythmical patterning of the picture surface can exist on as many levels as the differentiations of the visual field. If a surface permits any subdivision that repeats its own shape or size in a smaller form, a simple geometrical order is achieved. This subdivision implies sizes, positions, directions and intervals. On this level there can be rhythm through regular alternating or orderly repeating shapes, positions, length, angles, curves, directions, intervals. When the orderly measure of the optical units is related to their virtual movement from and to the picture-plane a higher level of rhythm is reached. We have then a rhythm of the plastic forces, a regular change of sensation of spatial movements of colors and values; advancing, receding, expanding, contracting, moving up, down, left and right. Finally we might have orderly changes or repetition of more complex configurations of visual experience; rhythmic order of tension and repose, concentration and rarefaction, harmony and discord. Rhythm may be simple, restricted to one or another metre of the optical differences. It may also be compounded, as two or more lawfully varying metres existing simultaneously. Rhythms may correspond with and amplify each other, or they may oppose each other, causing a higher level of rhythmic configuration.

There is scarcely a culture in which the visual rhythm was not conceived at least in one form or another. In the past, however, the main interest has been concentrated on a static scale of geometric proportion. Rhythm was not understood as an organic result of dynamic sensory organization, but was regarded as the representation of certain absolute metres observed in visible nature or derived by mathematical speculations. Certain proportions observed in the human body, in crystal formations, in leaves, have been borrowed and used, through corresponding subdivisions of the picture surface. Rhythms of growth and function foreign from the growth and function of the visual organization were frozen on the picture surface. Rhythm, in terms of geometric measure only, neglected the dynamic quality of visual experience, the movements of the plastic forces.

54

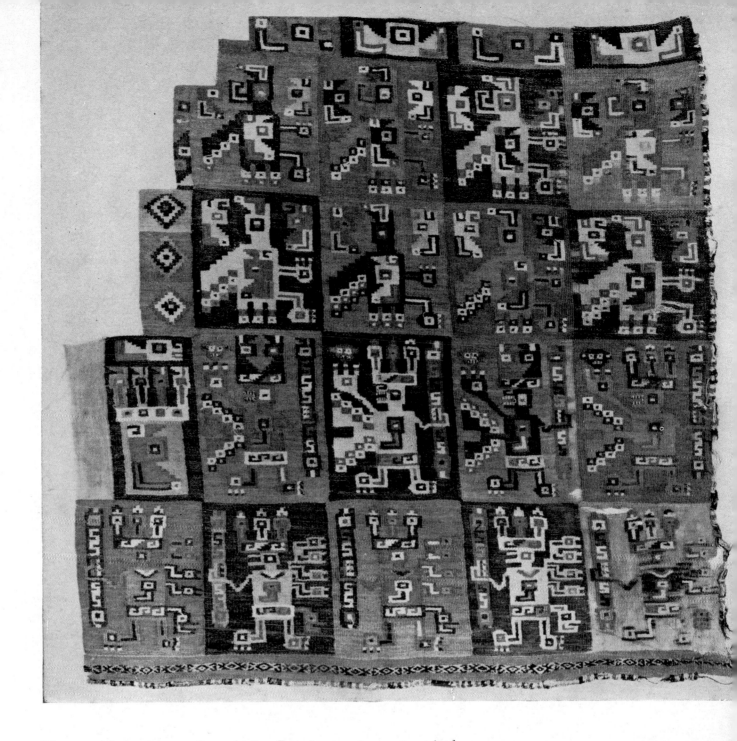

There were, however, exceptions. Ancient Peruvian tapestry was conceived in a healthy respect for the rhythm intrinsic in the dynamic process of visual organization. By a careful interchange of the lines, shapes, colors, the rhythm of time is translated into space. These designs are described by Franz Boas, who says:

"On many fabrics we find patterns consisting of a diagonal arrangement of squares or rectangles. In each diagonal the same design is repeated, while the next diagonal has another type. In each diagonal line the design is shown in varying positions. If the one faces the right, the next faces the left. At the same time there is an alternation of colors, so that even when the form is the same, the tints and the color values will not be the same."

Seurat. *Le Chahut 1890*
Courtesy of The Albright Art Gallery, Buffalo

After the sterile, static approach to the rhythmic ordering of the picture surface, Seurat in the last century brought rhythm back to a dynamic level. He welded shapes, directions, colors, sizes, into a rhythmic unity by a carefully planned inter-action of horizontal, vertical directions, straight and curvular lines, and the advancing and receding movements of the colors.

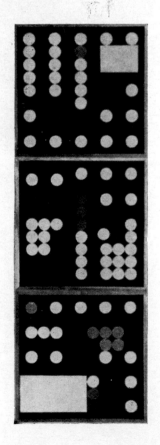

Sophie Taeuber-Arp. *Composition 1931*

Mondrian and Doesburg carried this dynamic principle of rhythm to final purification and maximum intensity. By reducing the picture surface to the basic opposites—pure colors, elementary shapes, and horizontal and vertical directions—by eliminating any resemblance to the familiar object world, as Mondrian writes, art today has succeeded in establishing a plastic expression, "the clear realization of liberated and universal rhythm distorted and hidden in the individual rhythm of the limiting form."

The invention of the motion picture opened the way to a hitherto undreamed scope and flexibility of rhythmic organization. The new possibilities of the synchronization of the temporal and spatial structure of the vision are, however, still barely touched upon. From the few pioneers who tackled the problems, Viking Eggeling and Hans Richter made the first and most important practical and theoretical clarifications. Eggeling pointed to the very core of all visual organization when he wrote, "What should be grasped and given form are things in flux."

58

Organization of spatial progression. The equivocal space

Rhythmic organization, although an essential condition for keeping the attention and thus prolonging the life span of the image, is not in itself fully sufficient to secure the maximum endurance of attention necessary for integration of a plastic form. One is well acquainted with the irritating sensation produced by the regular repetition of a sound of a drum. One knows almost instinctively that a simple rhythmic pattern possesses a regularity that soon becomes monotony. If the image is to remain a living organism, the relationships within it must have progressively changing aspects. One cannot long look at the same visual relationship without exhausting nervous energies of attention. The power of rhythm in keeping attention prolonged is conditioned by the necessity to feed attention by progressively changing optical material. Change implies movement. The final task of plastic organization is, then, the creation of an optical structure of movement that will dictate the direction and progression of plastic relationships until the experience reaches full integration. The most evident characteristic of movement is its unity, its dynamic continuity. Movement, however, implies also the opposite of unity: variety of locations. The very meaning of movement lies in this inner contradiction of the dynamic unity and the static discontinuity. To experience movement, then, means to disclose its contradictory aspects, to establish their mutual relationships, to follow up the contradiction through all stages. The picture field is two-dimensional surface and the optical changes therefore must necessarily be within the circulation of the vision on the flat plane. The kinetic basis of plastic organization—the linear paths of the eye on the picture-plane—is the common measure that binds into a unity the changing plastic relationships. The eye follows the given path, and the kinetic sensation of the eye movement charges the line with its own experience-quality and establishes a dynamic continuity, a unity of the surface.

The function of the kinetic linear path in plastic organization may be compared with the function of melody in musical composition, and the following observations of musicians should be helpful in bringing about further clarification.

"Music, theoretically considered, consists altogether of lines of tone. It more nearly resembles a picture or an architectural drawing, than any other art creation; the difference being that in a drawing the lines are visible and constant, while in music they are audible and in motion. The separate tones are the points through which the lines are drawn; and the impression which is intended, and which is apprehended by the intelligent listener, is not that of single tones, but of continuous lines of tones, describing movements, curves and angles, rising, falling, poising—directly analogous to the linear impressions conveyed by a picture or drawing."●

●P. Goetschius, Elementary Counterpoint

59

This linear unity can encompass all possible optical opposites on all levels of space and can be generated by any factor of visual organization. When plastic forces fail to create the experience of depth, linear movement will organize flat shapes. Not only does each shape have its own individuality, but simultaneously the outlines of the shapes have dynamic power to lead the eye from one to another. A number of contiguous shapes placed on the picture-plane are automatically connected by the movement of their continuous outlines. These lines move first from one figure to another, forming groups, and then from one group to another, creating a progressive organization of all the elements on the picture surface. The common dynamic linear direction thus has an equivocal meaning. Each shape outline shares the direction of visual flow. This ambiguous spatial content is increased in vitality when new qualities are added to the shapes. If value differences are introduced where value uniformity previously held, if one shape is made black and another white, the remaining ones of intermediary values, the two-fold character of the space will be made more evident. One shape will appear to advance toward the spectator, another to recede, and so on, but the evident or latent continuation of the outline continues to move on the flat surface and the contradiction and identity between the depth dimensions and the picture-plane are brought to life. This two-fold characteristic can be still further increased by the addition of color, texture and other spatial qualities and by the illusory indication of form or action.

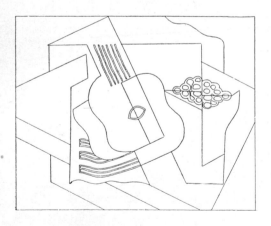

Linear diagram of a
Painting by **Juan Gris**

Directions of the visual flow on the surface can also be indicated in more subtle ways. A kind of psychological filling-in of the optical intervals will supply latent lines capable of performing the same role of organization as actual lines for shapes which have in their own right no common lines whatsoever. According to the law of closure, intervals of colors and values can emerge into forms, intervals of lines into shapes, intervals of points into lines, generating new figures with new kinetic outlines.

The study of certain optical situations where the attention fluctuates between figure and background, and where each in turn emerges as the figure or the background, makes it evident that there is no fundamental difference, in an optical sense, between the figure and the background, between the positive and negative space. Linear movement is based not only upon the activity of existing lines or outlines of figures, but also upon the latent outlines of the intervals between these figures.

The kinetic outlines of the figures generated by the optical intervals constitute an integral part of the plastic organization. They live, act, and move with the same kinetic power as the lines and shapes intentionally created.

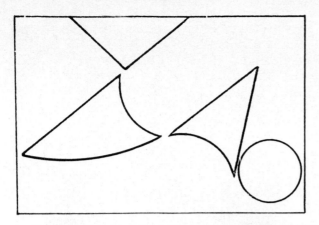

Carlotta Corpron. *Light Volumes*
Linear Continuance of Value Graduations

62

Picasso. *Seated Woman 1927*
Reproduction Courtesy of the Art Institute of Chicago.

Sano Di Pietro. *Madonna And Child*
Courtesy of The Smith College Museum of Art

Plastic movement can be repeated in various visual qualities such as color, tone value, texture, shape, form, and so on. The eye passing from one sensory stimulation to another receives an accumulated impetus which leads it to embrace newer relationships on the picture surface.

Music suggests an excellent analogy. A musical unit played by an instrument is repeated contrapuntally on other instruments, on the strings, on the brasses, on the woodwinds, even on percussion instruments. Each plastic unit with its specific sensory quality echoes the previous one; light, dark, color, shapes, forms, all mutually help one another, one taking over the movement where another stopped, leading toward complete unity.

"The groups of tones in a melody which are harmonically connected are like the links of a chain; they give the melody color and sheen. They are the real body of the melody, strange as it may seem to speak of body in connection with a linear phenomenon like a melody. It must not be forgotten that a melody is only primarily linear, and that the comparison with a curved line applies only to the most obvious, external aspect of a chain of tones. The melodic thread has an ever-changing but ever-present volume or thickness."

*Hindemith, Craft of Musical Composition

63

Nicolas Poussin. *Drawing*

The finest example of spatial orchestration by movement within the limitations of classical object representations was achieved by Poussin.

Nicolas Poussin. *Triumph of Bacchus*

Courtesy of
The William Rockhill Nelson Gallery of Art

64

II. *Visual Representation*

In the foregoing chapter, we considered the plastic image as a living organism, the laws of its growth and structure. Such a living organism is rooted in nature and depends upon the visible nature for its food. For a fuller understanding of the image, its role, and its effectiveness, we must learn its relationship to the visible features of our changing environment.

Man is a dynamic being struggling individually and socially for survival. To survive he must orient himself to his surroundings. He must measure and order the visual impacts of his environment to correspond with nature. He must communicate his findings to his fellow men for the mutual reinforcement of their actions. He asserts himself in the material world by means of his sensory equipment as well as his thinking process. Thus the control of nature includes the domestication of nature through the eye, the visual assimilation of space-time events.

Visual images are tools for this progressive control of nature. Each new visual conquest creates a new horizon, a new frame of reference, a new starting point for further development. As the aspects of nature change, man needs to readjust these tools and develop new uses for them. As there is progress of the thinking process, so also there is evolution of sensory comprehension. The development of vision leads not only to further understanding of nature but also to the progressive development of human sensibilities, and thus to wider and deeper human experiences.

It is common experience that activities originally voluntary become with practice largely automatic. Arriving in a new town, one is conscious of every step one takes. Orientation is a voluntary activity, each step involving a conscious measuring of distance and direction. But with familiarity orientation becomes mechanical. One goes from place to place without conscious thought of route or landmarks. Sitting for the first time behind the wheel of an automobile, one must give concentrated voluntary attention to every motion of hand and foot. In time, however, these manipulations become automatic. The driver may talk or listen to the radio without being afraid of losing control of the car. The act of talking requires complex coordination of muscles and vocal chords. Yet in conversation we are primarily aware of the meanings we wish to express and hardly conscious at all of the tongue and lip movements we use to form the sounds and convey the meaning.

As William James says:

"The great thing, then, in all education is to make our nervous system an ally instead of an enemy. It is to fund and capitalize our acquisitions and live at ease upon the interests of the fund. For this we must make automatic and habitual as early as possible as many useful actions as we can. . . . The more of the details of our daily life we can hand over to the effortless custody of automatism, the more the higher power of mind will be set free for their own proper work."

We see as the painters, sculptors, architects, photographers, advertising designers teach us to see. The social value of the representational image is, therefore, that it may give us education for a new standard of vision. The voluntary action of the painter, as he strives to make terms with the changing aspects of space-time events, must be translated through the objective image in the beholder's experience into a new and automatic standard of vision.

Seeing spatial relationships on a flat land is a different experience from seeing them in a mountain region where one form intercepts the other. To orient oneself in walking requires a different spatial measurement than does riding in a motor-car or an aeroplane. To grasp spatial relationships and orient oneself in a metropolis today, among the intricate dimensions of streets, subways, elevated trains, and skyscrapers, requires a new way of seeing.

As the Euclidean geometry was but a first approximation in the knowledge of spatial forms, reflecting only a certain limited complex of spatial properties, the traditional forms of visual representation were but the first approximation in sensing the spatial reality.

In the last hundred years technological practice has introduced a new, complex visual environment. The contemporary painter's task is to find the way of ordering and measuring this new world. This historical challenge calls him to assimilate the new findings and to develop a new sensibility, a new standard of vision that can release the nervous system to a broader scale of orientation.

Visual representation operates by means of a sign system based upon a correspondence between the sensory stimulations and the visible structure of physical world. Space-time events of the physical world must be translated into the relationships of color surfaces on the picture-plane. Man has gradually learned to order certain visible relationships of space-time events; that is, of extent, of depth, and of movement. The historical development of representation shows a gradual conquest of these optical relationships in the terms of the two-dimensional picture surface.

This optical correspondence is by no means necessarily congruent with the spatial experience intrinsic in a plastic organization of the picture surface. A photograph of a running horse may appear inert within the four boundaries of the picture-plane, if its position, frozen on the picture-plane, has a plastic relationship with the two-dimensional surface which gives a static experience. The same photograph will be dynamic if the optical units are so ordered in reference to the picture margins as to induce a kinetic experience. It is necessary to find a congruency between these two frames of reference: the observed relationships in the actual spatial world and the spatial nature of the two-dimensional picture-plane. A visual representation of nature can be vital in human experience only if it becomes a nature form itself by reaching an organic quality, a plastic unity.

The goal is a visual representation in which the most advanced knowledge of space is synchronized with the nature of the plastic experience. Space-time is order, and the image is an "orderer." Only the integration of these two aspects of order can make the language of vision what it should be: a vital weapon of progress.

Visual representation has three parallel tendencies. The first is the tendency to approximate in a two-dimensional relationship the totality of spatial experience. It is a synthesis which includes, not only what one sees but what one knows about the thing seen. If one knows that a man has two legs, then he will draw them both, although only one leg be seen from the particular angle of observation. If one knows that a plate has a circular shape and a characteristic local color, he will represent that plate in its characteristic visual form, although from his particular angle of vision the plate must appear elliptical, and its color be changed by variable illumination. The conceptual characteristics of the spatial units, rather than the apparent optical characteristics, are shown. The second tendency is toward the most precise graphic recording of objects projected on the retina. The artist tries to put on a flat surface one apparent optical aspect of the mobile, spatial world. The third tendency is toward a representation of the content of desire and will. The selection and arrangement of representational elements are guided by the artist's desire to bring release from emotional tensions by materializing in the symbolic forms of representation the objectives of his wishes.

The history of visual representation shows a changing emphasis now on one, now on another, of these components. The representational image is never identical with the spatial reality, but approximates it according to the prevailing standards of interest and knowledge. One does not see every aspect of visible things and events; one selects and arranges the visual stimulations according to one's attitude toward these things. To the same degree that the knowledge of the environment and the habits and attitudes toward the environment change, the visual habits of representation also change.

A revaluation of representation idioms comes about only when new elements that invade the environment field are important enough to demand attention and when there are no traditions to shape visual habits in regard to them. The recent changes in science and technology demand such revaluation. New experiences, scientific, technological, and social, do not fit any longer into the old frame of reference. As our concept of reality deepens and our knowledge of space widens, a fundamental revaluation of the traditional forms of representation is unavoidable. The re-checking of the idioms of space-representation and their integration with the genuine language of the picture surface is the vital task of the contemporary artist. The following sections survey the inherited idioms of visual representation and evaluate them in contemporary terms.

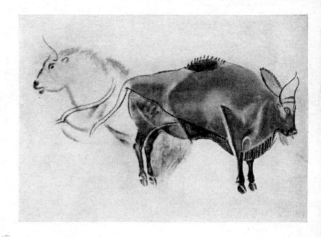

The single unit

The narrowest form of spatial grasp is the perception of the single spatial unit. The simplest form of spatial representation is that of a single spatial element.

Primitive man had a limited understanding of space and time. For him, each experience was confined to its own space-time life, without reference to past or future or wider spatial relationships. He felt little, if any, need for comparing and measuring. His visual representation was limited, for the most part, to single spatial units. The visual comprehension of the figures he represented was not connected with the understanding of the surrounding space. He was little concerned with backgrounds, weight, top or bottom. Each element lived its own life in complete spatial independence. Represented figures were only transitory on the picture surface. The figure and the background were not in organic interdependence. This unframed character of the picture surface, the lack of a spatial frame of reference, may be the reason that prehistoric artists frequently overlapped with new paintings the work of their predecessors. Children's drawing reveals a similar attitude. Spatial elements are not yet grasped in their inter-connections. They have no unified frame of reference. Because there is no coherent spatial background to which to relate the elements, drawings on a picture-plane have only accidental organization. Children draw until the figure reaches the limits of the paper. Then they turn the paper over and fill in the available space.

70

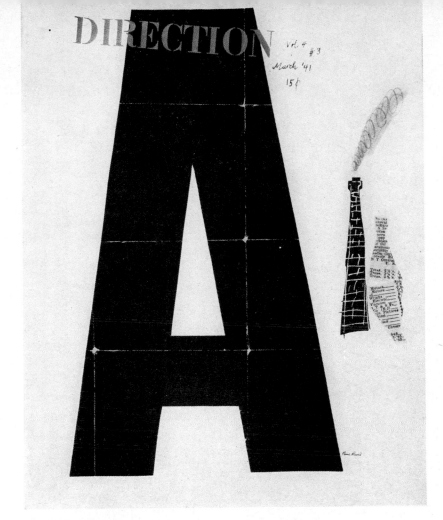

Advertising Design 1941
Paul Rand.

Relationship of size

We are accustomed to attribute to a larger retinal projection spatial emphasis, that is, a larger space-filling characteristic. Size, therefore, becomes the simplest statement about space—the first step of organization of the spatial world.

In early forms of visual representation, space is indicated by the extension of the color areas on the picture surface. In these early representational images, the hierarchy of size was intimately associated with the hierarchy of power. strength, and importance. Thus, the first spatial scale had a structural correspondence to the scale of values. Size relationships were used not only as a spatial sign but also as symbols and as a means of plastic emphasis.

Renaissance perspective destroyed this structural correspondence of space, symbol, and plastic emphasis by a slavish imitation of the apparent optical image of the three-dimensional object-world. After a long eclipse, this structural use of size differences was rediscovered by contemporary painters, photographers and motion picture camera men. Advertising art, uninhibited by tradition, also found a dynamic and structural use of the contrasting size of color surfaces. The page has its own spatial world, not in a naturalistic sense as an illusion of actual distances between the represented elements, but in the sense that in it the size of picture and word are in a plastic and meaningful connection.

Relationship of depth by vertical location

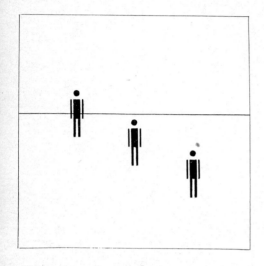

For the spectator, the horizon line provides a frame of reference. He judges the position of the object he sees in relation to the horizon line, and so receives an impression of its distance from himself as well as from other objects before him. Even if the horizon line is not apparent, the different elevations of the elements indicate a position in depth.

Representation on the two-dimensional picture surface has conventionally utilized the spatial meaning of the vertical location. The visible or latent horizon line was kept as the frame of reference. The picture-plane has been identified with, and conventionally fixed to, the horizontal ground plane. The bottom of the picture-plane has represented the closest visual point; consequently the degree of elevation of the visual units indicated receding spatial positions.

K'o Ssu. *Feast of the Peaches*
Courtesy of The Minneapolis Institute of Arts

Aerial Photograph

Kasimir Malevich.
Suprematist Composition
1914

Ladislav Sutnar. *Photograph*

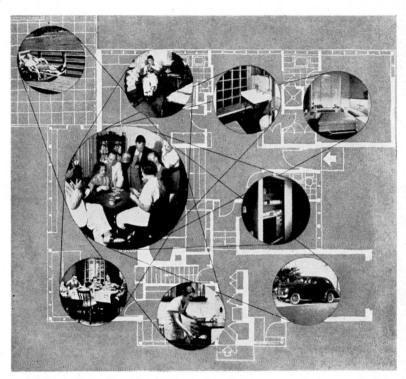

William Burtin. *Advertising Design 1941*

Ladislav Sutnar. *Book Jacket 1930*

New technological discoveries have brought about a fundamental revaluation of vertical position as a sign of depth. Bird's-eye view and frog's-eye view in photographs and a new vision in aerial observation were the most important factors. For the airman, as well as for the photographer, the horizon line changes constantly, and consequently loses its absolute validity. No longer was it inevitable that the visual understanding of objects and their spatial relationships be based upon a frame of reference which had a constant—the fixed visible or latent horizon.

Thus freed, the signs of space representation can function as plastic forces. The order of actual space and the space of the picture-plane are in close congruency.

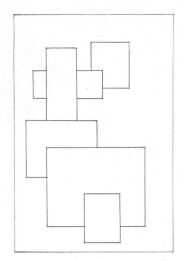

Representation of depth by overlapping figures

If one spatial form obstructs our view of another form, we do not assume that the second ceases to exist because it is hidden. We recognize, as we look at such overlapping figures, that the first or uppermost has two spatial meanings—itself and beneath itself. The figure which intercepts the visible surface of another figure is perceived as nearer. We experience spatial differences or depth. Representation of overlapping indicates depth. It creates a sense of space. Each figure appears parallel with the picture-plane and tends to establish a receding spatial relationship.

Last Judgment

German 1460

Reproduction Courtesy
The Art Institute of Chicago

76

Clifford Eitel.

Study of transparency

*Work done for the author's course
in Visual Fundamentals*

*Sponsored by
The Art Director's Club of Chicago*

*"Migrating billiard balls cannot
pass through one another: en-
counter means displacement. But
migrating waves from different
centers (as on the surface of a
pond) can pass through one another without conflict, adding
themselves to one another as they
pass. And ordinarily, two gases,
released into the same closed
space, will expand through one
another until each fills the entire
space. In the physical world there
are numerous examples of 'interpretation.' Is it conceivable
that political expansions might
also interpenetrate like waves,
rather than collide like billiard
balls?" —William Ernest Hock-
ing. America's World Purpose.*

Transparency, interpenetration

If one sees two or more figures partly overlapping one another, and each
of them claims for itself the common overlapped part, then one is
confronted with a contradiction of spatial dimensions. To resolve this
contradiction, one must assume the presence of a new optical quality.
The figures are endowed with transparency; that is, they are able to
interpenetrate without an optical destruction of each other. Transparency however implies more than an optical characteristic; it implies
a broader spatial order. Transparency means a simultaneous perception
of different spatial locations. Space not only recedes but fluctuates in a
continuous activity. The position of the transparent figures has equivocal
meaning as one sees each figure now as the closer, now as the further one.

The order of our time is to knead together the scientific and technical
knowledge acquired, into an integrated whole on the biological and social
plane. Today there are hardly any aspects of human endeavor where the
concept of interpenetration as a device of integration is not in focus. Technology, philosophy, psychology, and physical science are using it as
a guiding principle. So do literature, painting, architecture, motion
picture and photography, and stage design. Furthermore, it is a com-
monplace technical knowledge in our everyday life. Radio waves are
the clearest example of this.

Picasso. *Portrait of Kahnweiler*
Courtesy of Mrs. Charles B. Goodspeed

Amadee Ozenfant. *Purist Still Life*
Courtesy of Art of This Century

G. F. Keck. *Detail of a House*
Photograph by W. Keck

Contemporary architecture utilizes the transparent quality of synthetic materials, glass, plastics, etc., to create a design that will integrate the greatest possible number of spatial vistas. Inside and outside are in close relationship, and each viewpoint in the building offers the widest visible comprehension of space. Reflections and mirrorings, transparent and translucent building materials are carefully calculated and organized to focus divergent spatial vistas in one visual grasp.

L. Moholy Nagy.
Space Construction 1930

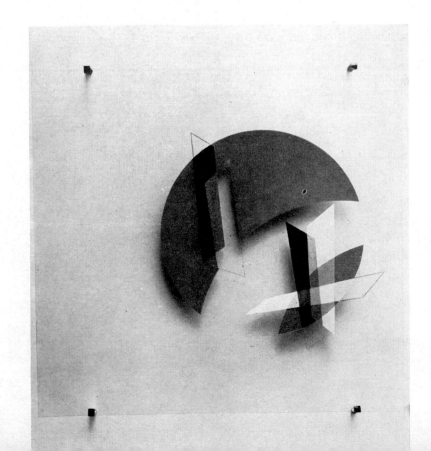

79

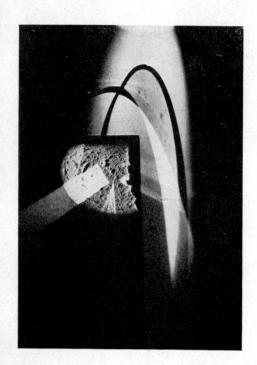

Technical control of artificial light-sources, the projection of images by light, has contributed also to the revaluation of overlapping and the introduction of the representational device of transparency. Light rays covering an image are able to interpenetrate one another, light increases light, shadow deepens shadow. The result is greater intensity.

The photographic emulsion is characteristically able to record on one picture surface two or more superimposed projections. The resulting effect compresses two or more spatial aspects and moulds them into a broader type of space representation. X-ray photography opened up a new aspect of the visible world. Things hitherto hidden from the human eye could be penetrated and made visible. Here the transparency has a new meaning, because the depth of the object is also evaluated by its optical density.

Gyorgy Kepes. *Photomontage 1937*

Gyorgy Kepes. *Advertising Design 1937*

William Burtin. *Advertising Design 1940*

Jack Waldheim. *Superimposed Photography 1943*

Paul Rand. *Poster Project*

Frank Barr. *Typographical Design 1941*

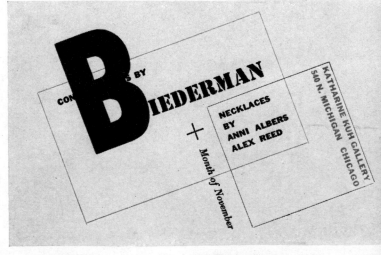

Cassandre. *Air Orient 1932*

Courtesy of The Museum of Modern Art

The technique of the printing process offers another opportunity for the creative control of transparency. One printing over another will condense a variety of spatial dimensions into one meaningful whole.

Cover Design 1934

E. McKnight Kauffer. *Poster*

Courtesy of The Museum of Modern Art

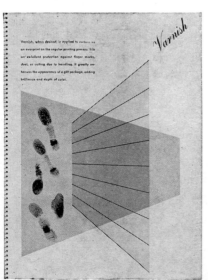

Gyorgy Kepes. *Advertising Design 1938*

Le Corbusier, *Drawing*
Courtesy of Carl O. Schniewind

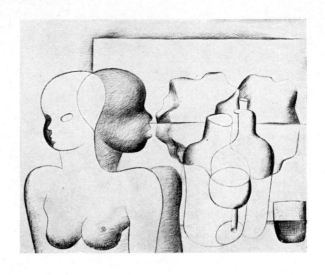

Fernand Leger, *Advertising Design 1942*
Courtesy of Container Corporation of America

Linear perspective

The retinal image of the objects shrinks or swells as the objects are closer to or further from the spectator. Helmholtz says:

> The same object seen at different distances will be depicted on the retina by images of different sizes and will subtend different visual angles. The further it is away the less its apparent size will be. Thus just as astronomers can compute the variations of the distances of the sun and moon from the changes in the apparent sizes of these bodies, so knowing the size of the object, a human being for instance, we can estimate the distance from us by means of the visual angle subtended or, what amounts to the same thing, by means of the size of the image on the retina.

The use of this geometrical relationship was re-introduced by the Renaissance painters as the main device for representing spatial relationships. Their artistic goal was the optical scientific mastery of nature. Conditioned by the aspirations and outlook of the Renaissance, they sought to achieve this step by step by focusing always on one aspect, on one cut-out sector, of the unbounded wealth of surrounding nature. Like the anatomist—another pioneer of the same spirit, who made his conquest of knowledge by eliminating the living, moving aspects of the body—the artist—anatomist of the visual image—eliminated the flux of the innumerable visual relationships that the visible world has for the spectator. He froze the living, fluctuating wealth of the visual field into a static geometrical system, eliminating the time-element always present in the experiencing of space, and thus destroying the dynamic relationships in the experience of the spectator.

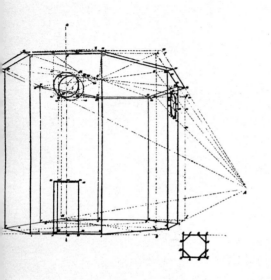

Perspective drawing by
Piero della Francesco

Inverse perspective

In accordance with the ancient Chinese canons, Chinese and Japanese painters assign to linear perspective a diametrically opposite role from that given it by western painters. In their system parallel lines converge as they approach the spectator. They open up the space instead of closing it. The picture space is not a scientific optical diagram of the apparent positions of objects but a medium of experience, an active two-dimensional panorama for the spectator, who lives the image. The same approach was used in many early European paintings.

Early German Woodcut

Jere Donovan,
Photomontage. Action

Herbert Bayer Design Class 1939

Sponsored by
The American Advertising Guild

Linear perspective gave a unified formulation of space, but it restricted the spatial relationships to one angle of vision, one fixed point of view, that of the spectator, by creating an illusory depth between the objects and an illusory distortion of their actual shape. An unimportant detail can intercept in a foreshortened image the most significant element, thus making the whole unintelligible. We may blot out a house or a man by holding a finger close to the eye. From a certain angle of view, dissimilar forms may appear as similar optical projections and similar forms as dissimilar.

If any meaning of depth is to flow from foreshortening and diminishing by the use of perspective, the observer must be acquainted with the objects in their actual three-dimensional characteristics. A memory constancy, moreover, is attached to familiar things of our surroundings. We keep a constant size and shape in our perception however the size and shape of the retinal projection may vary with changes in our angle of vision. For example, when we see two men, one six feet away and the other fifteen, they both appear to us approximately the same size. When we look at a plate from an oblique angle, it should, by the rules of linear perspective, appear elliptical; actually we still see it as round. When we look, the retinal projection fixes on only a small fragment of the spatial relationship that we actually perceive; we supplement the unseen part with our memory constant of a unified spatial background.

Size differences which do not register in direct visual perception and appear unchanged although they project different images on the retina reveal, when fixed on a two-dimensional picture-plane, a great power to accentuate the illusion of depth between objects.

Tintoretto, *Hercules and Antaeus*
Courtesy of Wadsworth Atheneum

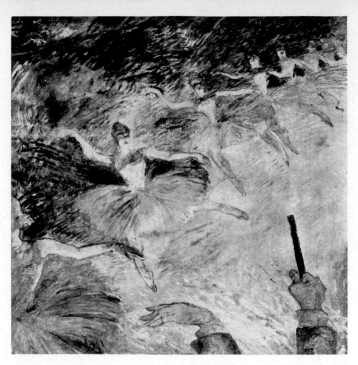

Toulouse-Lautrec, *Ballet Dancers*
Courtesy of The Art Institute of Chicago

Amplified perspective

Almost as soon as the Renaissance introduced perspective, its painters began to find the fixed system of space representation less than satisfying. Some attempted to break the bonds by going to extremes. The unified space of the linear perspective was saturated by extreme distortions. The maximum contrast of small and large was applied to inject the picture space with the optimum of vitality. The perspective framework was stretched or condensed to the utmost limits, reaching the greatest dynamic expression possible within the static linear-perspective system.

Amplified perspective is used in photography, photomontage and in motion picture as a potent device for creating a strong sense of space.

A. M. Cassandre, *Poster 1932*
Courtesy of The Museum of Modern Art

89

Multiple, simultaneous perspective

Other painters modified and disrupted the static spatial unity of the linear perspective by introducing into one picture a number of vanishing points and several horizons. Their aim was to bring into the picture space the widest possible spatial relationship, instinctively moulding the linear perspective to the nature of the picture-plane. Leonardo da Vinci, in his Adoration, introduced a number of points of view and several horizon lines to make the landscape in the background clearly visible. Jan Van Eyck sometimes used three or more vanishing points to increase the inner space of a room. Veronese, Tintoretto, and other painters employed in one picture many vanishing points and horizon lines.

Their work was the first to break with the limited system of linear perspective which made the spectator pause in time and in space—a contradiction to the nature of visual experience. By multiple perspective, the static fixation was overcome, because simultaneous perspective means moving in space.

Di Paolo. *Baptist in the Wilderness*
Courtesy of The Art Institute of Chicago

Tintoretto, *Venus and Mars with Three Graces*
Courtesy of The Art Institute of Chicago

Mechanical perfection of the linear perspective

Vision unchained by the photographic camera was able to explore hitherto untouched territories of perspective. Latent optical aspects became apparent because the camera was able to reproduce objects from an angle of vision that the unaided eye could not achieve in reasonable comfort, if at all. Not only the accustomed frontal and profile-views but also the view from above, the bird's-eye view, and that from below, the frog's-eye view, were recorded. The vanishing point which, in the traditional space representation, had usually been in the middle of the picture-plane was shifted left, right, up and down, into almost all possible positions. For each changing position there was not only a corresponding cut-out of the visual field but also, within this cut-out, a different foreshortening.

Motion picture photography still further increased the elasticity of foreshortening and introduced a hitherto unseen flexibility in the use of size differences for space accentuation. The "closeup" broke up the traditional continuous space unity inherited through painting and theatre and extended the picture space to amplified dimension. In a sequence a "closeup," "medium shot," and "long shot" bring a living, moving variety of expanding and condensing space.

Optical accessories within or outside the camera were employed for the further exploration of the appearances of things. Mirrors, prisms, and special lenses sketched, diffused, distorted, repeated, moulded the things and created images not corresponding to direct visual perception.

L. Moholy Nagy,
Bauhaus in Dessau 1926
Spring 1929
Bird's Eye View 1925

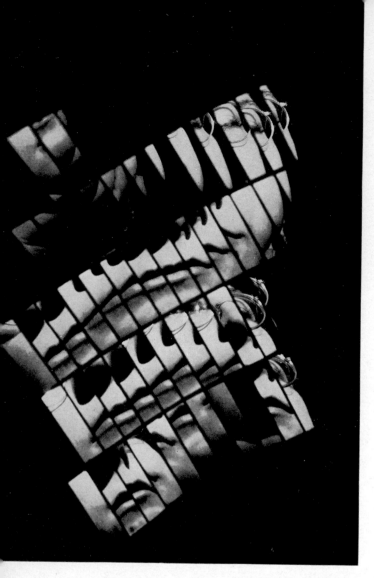

George Morris,
Distortion by Prism 1940 •

M. Halberstadt, *Mirroring 1941* •

• *Experimental work done under the direction of the
author in the Light and Color Department*
School of Design in Chicago.

James Brown,
Distortion in Mirror 1940

Breakdown of fixed perspective

The invention and perfection of the camera was by no means the only factor tending to break down the absolute validity of linear perspective. The whole social trend of the contemporary world made such breakdown inevitable.

The Renaissance, which re-discovered the rules of that perspective, had awakened economic forces which led to an interest in every facet of understanding and control of nature. This interest, in turn, released tremendous scientific and technological progress. The progress revolutionized production and reshaped the economic and social structure and transformed man's inner and outer landscape.

The new technical devices, machines, were able to produce and reproduce, with hitherto unknown speed and in a hitherto undreamed of quantity, objects, commodities for human use. All human efforts were concentrated on producing objects. The human being himself became lost in his own evaluation of an object able to produce another object. The mechanical nature of the whole social and economic existence was assimilating man. It was breaking into the human sphere and destroying it. He became a machine, or a part of a machine. Man was losing his status as an individual. In his own life, the illusory laws of individual perspective was being destroyed by uncontrolled mechanization. The apparent economic space of the individual—his belief in his ability to make his own life, guided only by his own interest, will and force— was being broken up by economic mechanism.

The complexity of the product outgrew human control. The wealth of production became unusable and wasted because of the lack of social understanding, that is, planned direction. The new objects and new devices had brought to the visual field a wealth of new material. There were a thousand new things to see and a thousand new ways of seeing, but most of these were also wasted because there was no ordering principle established to organize the new visible world.

Faced with this situation, the individual tried to master it. He protested against being just another object, and he searched for his position in space. Painters, themselves drawn into the conflict, used the image as a testing ground, a battlefield. They forced their interest on the object and on its position in space. They had to master and to understand the spatial characteristics of objects in order to understand themselves, and so redirect their own lives.

Space analysis of the object

An individual confronted with a new complex task seeks at once for some form of precedent to aid him. He makes an inventory of his past experience and that of others. Likewise, in critical times when a group is facing new, complex social or cultural problems, the solution of which is beyond habitual pattern, the first instinctive step is to look back for solutions and borrow wisdom from distant cultures.

In their search for a new structural order in which available wealth could function, contemporary painters, confused and cornered in this turmoil of the new visual environment, also rediscovered solutions from previous cultures. Negro sculpture from Africa gave, on a small scale one answer to their problem. In these simple forms each enveloping plane does not submerge in an illusory whole but acts as an individual dynamic direction leading to another plane which in turn leads to the understanding of the whole. Each plane, in its simplicity unhindered by details, has a clear dynamic structural function.

Picasso, *Dancer 1907*
Collection of
Walter P. Chrysler, Jr.

This dynamic idea of following up the planes enveloping an object was carried to further conclusions. Painters had discovered that one observation point, in spite of emphasis by distortion, was not sufficient to give the spatial essence of the object. So the painter moved around the object, penetrated it, and used all means available to describe the greatest possible number of its relationships to the spectator, and to other objects. All the sharpened tools of perspective were focused in one simultaneous representation. Painters shifted the point of vision into a kind of cinematographic sequence, and represented the projection of several points of view in one picture.

Russian Ikon, *St. Nikolai*
Hammer Galleries, New York

With the directness of a single-minded purpose, the drawings of primitive man always display the clearest way to state the essentials of a visible thing. When a primitive man uses a kind of X-ray picture to show essential spatial entity of things or when he uses simultaneously the profile and the face of a figure, he finds the very core of the representation-problem. The spectator is led on the picture surface to all the significant spatial references of the subject; the visual experience becomes a dynamic experience.

When a child attempts the graphic representation of a spatial situation, he is not satisfied with an accidental perspective projection. He twists and tilts the various possible visual aspects until he fully explains the objects he wishes to represent. The final result is a combination of plan and elevation. In drawing a cart, the child gives the horse, the wheels, and the persons the most characteristic projection. There is finally a fusion of the three-dimensional world and the two-dimensional picture-plane.

Early medieval painters often repeated the main figure many times in the same picture. Their purpose was to represent all possible relationships that affected him, and they recognized that this could be done only by a simultaneous description of various actions. This connectedness in meaning, rather than the mechanical logic of geometrical optics, is the essential task of representation. Franz Boas in his book "Primitive Art" gives a lucid summary of the core of the visual representation.

96

"It is easily intelligible that a profile view of an animal in which only one eye is seen and in which one whole side disappears may not satisfy as a realistic representation. The animal has two eyes and two sides. When it turns I see the other side; it exists and should be part of a satisfying picture. In a front view the animal appears foreshortened. The tail is invisible and so are the flanks; but the animal has a tail and flanks and they ought to be there. We are confronted with the same problem in our representations of maps of the world. In a map on Mercator projection, or in our planiglobes, we distort the surface of the globe in such a way that all parts are visible. We are interested only in showing, in a manner as satisfactory as possible, the interrelations between the parts of the globe. The same is true in orthogonal architectural drawings, particularly when two adjoining views taken at right angles to each other, are brought into contact, or in copies of designs in which the scenes or designs depicted on a cylinder, a vase, or a spherical pot are developed on a flat surface in order to show at a single glance the interrelations of the decorative forms. In drawings of objects for scientific study we may also sometime adopt a similar viewpoint, and in order to elucidate important relations, draw as though we were able to look around the corner or through the object. Different moments are represented in diagrams in which mechanical movements are illustrated and in which, in order to explain the operation of a device, various positions of moving parts are shown.

"In primitive art both solutions have been attempted: the perspective as well as that showing the essential parts in combinations. Since the essential parts are symbols of the object, we may call this method the symbolic one. I repeat that in the symbolic method those features are represented that are considered as permanent and essential, and that there is no attempt on the part of the draftsman to confine himself to a reproduction of what he actually sees at a given moment."

Mixed Perspective, *Child's Drawing*

Mixed Profile, *Child's Drawing*
From Helga Eng. Psychology of Children's Drawings

Bushman Painting

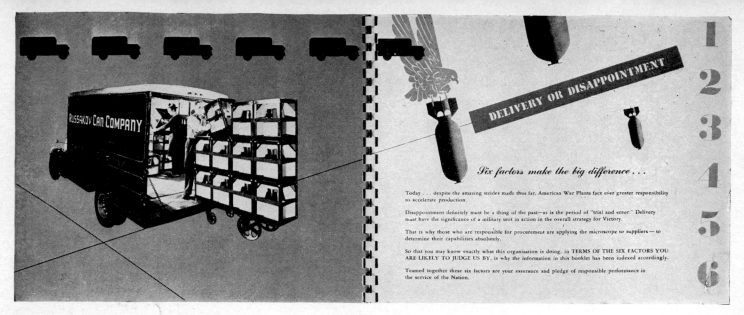

Morton Goldsholl. *Advertising Design 1943*

Advertising art, unhandicapped by traditional considerations, was free to develop a visual presentation in which every figure is pictured in the perspective which gives the strongest emphasis to its connectedness in a meaning.

Rediscovery of basic plastic forces: lines and color planes

The exploration of the spatial nature of the objects by walking—in imagination—around them, and investigating their visible volume made the image more formless. But in this formless conglomeration of the different enveloping planes, plastic forces hitherto hidden were revealed. Lines and shapes could now manifest a dynamic spatial quality which before had been submerged in the imitation of one apparent visual aspect.

The nature and limitations of the two-dimensional picture-plane, the specific plastic forces of color shapes due to their position and area, were again recognized as factors controlling the space building on this picture surface. "In art, progress lies not in an extension, but in a knowledge of limitations," said Braque. Instead of being derived straight from objects, shapes were moulded to fit the building of space on the picture-plane. The picture became an architecture of color planes created by the span between planes, and by their virtual movement from the picture surface. After the long period of cataloging the apparent aspects of nature, the spectator again became an integral part of the pictoral image. The image became once more a dynamic space experience instead of a dead inventory of optical facts.

Like the steel skeleton in architecture, which binds the walls into a spatial whole, the spatial span is achieved in the picture by the juxtaposition of lines and planes. When one plane moves by virtue of its color and shape in one direction, the linear structure juxtaposed to it brings it back.

This interlocking of planes and lines is an important step forward toward the rediscovery of the action of plastic forces. An unprecedented lightness is achieved, an open space-structure in which every movement can be followed clearly. The mass of the three-dimensional volumes and its gravitational one-sided movements are now exchanged for a dynamic space wherein the elements expand in every direction according to the mutual interactions of the receding or advancing color planes and the rhythmic flow of their lines.

Picasso,
Girl with Yellow Hat 1921
Collection of Walter P. Chrysler, Jr.

Paul Rand,
Advertising Design 1943

Integration of the plastic forces

The breaking up of the unifying system of linear perspective created two major difficulties. One was that the increasing number of spatial data were too numerous to include on the picture-plane. The other was that the plastic energies, liberated from the object and from the discipline of linear perspective, ran amok. To counteract these difficulties painters introduced two devices: first, the compression of planes through interpenetrations; and second, a rhythmical linear control of the picture surfaces.

Compression, interpenetration

The increasing number of points of reference brought exterior and interior, left and right, top and bottom of the object simultaneously before the eye. Only by extending the picture-plane to infinity could all visible aspects be simultaneously encompassed. Even if this were possible it would be no solution; for such an area would extend beyond the visual range. The limited area of the picture surface dictated the possible methods of bringing these many visible facts together. The search of the painters changed its direction from extension to concentration.

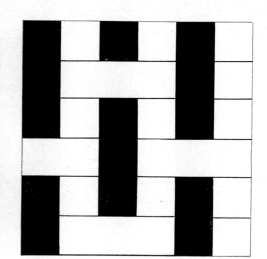

They began to compress the multitude of optical data within the confines of the picture surface by means of an interpenetration of one plane with another. They recognized, too, that color planes liberated from the object had a centrifugal action from the surface, and they sought to develop a balancing force which would bring order to this anarchy. The simplest form of integration they found was the interlocking of divergent elements, through a rhythmic interplay of opposing values, positive and negative. In weaving, the recurrence of the different colored threads creates unity by rhythmic discontinuity. The painters invented a similar device. By an interchange of opposing values, by analogy of opposites inside and out, black and white or contrasting colors, they were able to establish a common rhythm and consequently a unity. Plastic order was again achieved.

By interpenetration of different lines and planes, by interlocking of positive and negative, dark and light, a reciprocal action is produced. On a light surface dark lines or shapes, and on a dark surface light lines or shapes, become not only linked in a rhythmic discontinuity, but at the same time, by maximum contrast of each individual unit, achieve a greater intensity. The old Chinese sign gives a clear demonstration of a unity of opposites by the interdependence of each of its parts.

Braque, *Still Life on Table*
Chester Dale Collection
Courtesy of The Art Institute of Chicago

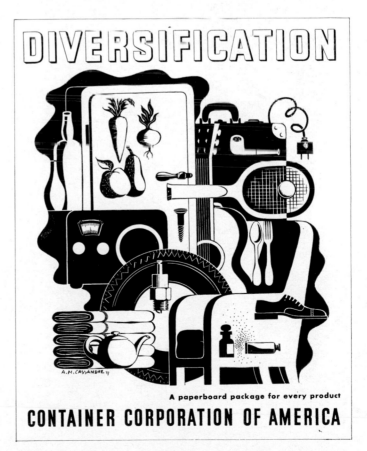

A. M. Cassandre, *Advertising Design 1937*
Courtesy of Container Corporation of America

Another device introduced for integration of the chaotic color planes was the use of a contour line common to the various spatial units. This common outline gains a double meaning like an optical pun. It refers to inside and outside space simultaneously, and the spectator is therefore forced into intensive participation as he seeks to resolve the apparent contradiction. But the equivocal contour line does more than unify different spatial data. It acts like a warp, weaving the threads of color planes into one rhythmical unity. This rhythmical flow of the line injects the picture surface with a sensual intensity.

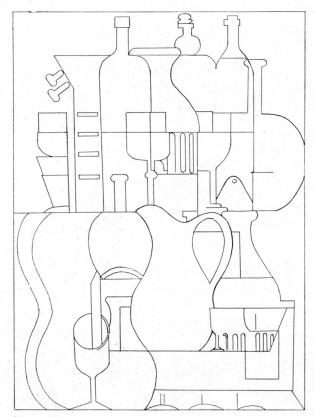

Linear diagram of a painting of **A. Ozenfant**

A. M. Cassandre, *Poster* Courtesy of The Museum of Modern Art

A. M. Cassandre, *Poster 1935*

The picture image employed for an advertising message has always posed the problem of bringing miscellaneous elements into harmonious fusion. Plastic and verbal elements operate on the same surface, each with its own force acting in its own direction. The copy, the calligraphic or mechanical quality of drawn elements, photography, colors, shapes, are different in their perspective, as well as in their plastic and associative meaning. To perceive the differences, one must compare the elements.

The contour of a face is an outline of a glass, a bottle, and also of a line of copy. The identical optical quality, the common contour line, creates a spatial unity, in the terms of the two-dimensional surface. Yet because it binds together the different elements, it forces comparison of their differences. These optical differences, through their inevitable contiguity, grow to be optical contradictions that can be resolved only in a new common meaning.

Jean Carlu, *Poster*

104

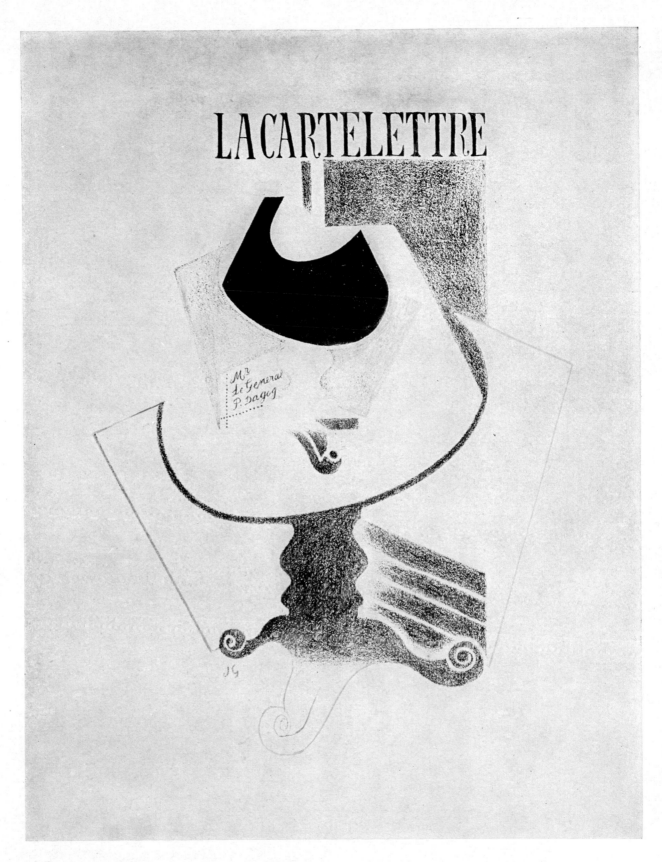

Juan Gris, *Lithograph "Jacob, Ne Coupez Pas Mademoiselle."* *Courtesy of The Museum of Modern Art*

G. Braque, *Painting*
Courtesy of Phillips Memorial Gallery

McKnight Kauffer, *Poster 1933*
Courtesy of The Museum of Modern Art

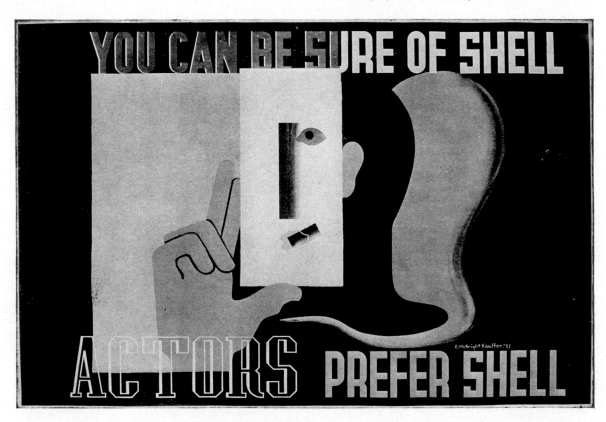

Cubist painters have only attempted a new visual formulation of the widened dimensions of the environment. They correctly realized that one fixed-perspective is not sufficient to describe dynamic spatial facts, and they experimented with numerous simultaneous perspective-projections. But the resulting picture image was still so closely associated with the old object-concept that it could not cover all possible space experience in contemporary life. The more complicated the environment and the greater the differences in experiences, the more necessary it became to find a simplification of the language. A visual language which would reduce to the lowest common denominator all experience, old and new, had still to be discovered. In a mathematical equation elements are eliminated and simplified until only the main structure of the equilibrium remains. The painters followed analogous procedure. From their visual "equation" they stripped all unessential elements. They reduced the image to its most elementary structure.

The work of the cubist painters only opened the road to a more controlled handling of the plastic forces on the picture surface. Their work only suggested that the picture has a life of its own, and that the plastic forces, lines, and planes, can create a spatial sensation without portraying objects. And the greater their departure from the object resemblance, the clearer the dynamic qualities of the plastic forces became. The bolder their attempt at an organization of these forces, the more apparent became the nature of the picture-plane, as entirely different from the illusory geometrical optical order of the object-world. The picture-plane was gradually recognized as a building having its own unique structural laws which could not be mingled or interchanged with the structural laws of the familiar object-world. Building with stone, wood, or reinforced concrete always has its respective structural requirements. Building on the two-dimensional surface with two-dimensional elements also demands its own handling. The efficiency and the strength of the picture image are dependent upon the correct estimates of the laws dictated by the two-dimensional medium employed.

The painters worked next to eliminate the remaining fragments of the object-representation, which they had come to regard as dead weight. The simplification had two poles. One was a successive elimination of all accidental characteristics of the picture units, a return to the basic geometrical elements—mainly to the rectangular shape—and to the straight line. The other was the search for the utmost possible precision in the relationship of these elements to each other and to the picture as a whole.

These inherent implications of the breaking-up of fixed perspective system crystallized into diametrically opposite developments. One occurred in Eastern Europe, where a final break was being made with the inherited patterns of social life, and where the tremendous reservoir of unused human and material resources was being released. The other took place in Western Europe—in Holland—where the turmoil of the last world war had least affected a peaceful development based on past standards, and where everything was concentrated on preserving the available conditions. The goals and directions of each corresponded to the character of the social background from which it emerged.

In Russia, Malevich, Rodchenko, Tatlin, El Lissitzky, and others carried on the explosive liberation of the plastic forces. Enjoyment of expanding and stretching space until matter was eliminated entirely was their motive power. The characteristic visual devices they used were the dynamic diagonal arrangement of the elements, their suspension in the background space, the empty void that absorbed them. This explosion into space necessarily lacked a clear order as a whole. The picture-plane was considered only as a point of departure.

In Holland, Doesburg and Mondrian were seeking to achieve the full compression of space, made possible by the limitation of the two-dimensional picture-plane. Their ideal was the most economic use of the plastic forces to bring out a dynamic balance from the receding and advancing of color planes and lines on the picture surface. Their work was based upon restriction, with equilibrium as the goal. They sought to order space in a perfectly measured relationship of color and line.

Their uncompromising analysis of the foundation of the plastic expression had a decisive influence on contemporary visual culture. From architecture to advertising-design there scarcely is any manifestation of visual activity that can avoid the implications of these two main trends.

Ultimate opening of the picture surface

Changing environment and new technological standards opened a new horizon of the visible world. To encompass these broader dimensions, the painters returned to the lowest common denominator of space representation. They rediscovered the spatial forces on the picture-plane, and their laws of organization inherent in the visual perception process, conditioned by the nature of a two-dimensional picture-plane. But the creative control of these laws was identified with space itself. Pure plastic sensation was dissociated from the visible environment from which it stems. The perfection of the instrument which could produce this sensation of space became a fetish—an independent value. Spatial experience was conceived only abstractly. As Malevich stated:

"All social ideas, great and important as they may be, are developing from the sensation of hunger; all works of art, small and insignificant as they may appear, emerge from a plastic sensation. There comes a time at last, to understand that the problems of art and the problems of the stomach and the reasons for each, are very different. Under suprematism, I understand the supremacy of pure sensation in the plastic arts . . . from the point of view of the suprematists, the appearance of the object-world is meaningless; the important thing being the sensation as such, independent of the circumstances."

The underlying philosophy of this final purification of the picture-plane from the object world led to ultimate rejection of any attempt to represent objective reality. "Everything we call nature, is, in the last analysis a fantasy picture," Malevich says, "with not the least resemblance to reality."

But as has been stated before, man asserts himself in the material world not only by means of thought but also by means of all his senses. Art is a sensuous form of consciousness, an important instrument in the conquest of nature, and representation is the creative assimilation of nature. The artistic conquest of space is not an end in itself, nor is it a matter of the senses alone. Herein lay the limitation of these pioneers of the language of vision. They had taken the first step toward freedom but they were hampered by lost faith in the integrated human existence. Their work was shaped in pseudomaterialism and resulted in isolationism—of sensory experience. The division of labor, dictated by shortsighted considerations, creating a one-sided individual, gave rise also to division within the individual, an inimical relationship of sense and reason. Instead of using the conquest of the senses for further integration of man with his surroundings, painters in their revolt against an involved and planless social system carried this fatal divison into the sphere of creative expression.

Because they worked with fierce honesty, however; because they were content with no half-measures, but gave themselves completely to the rediscovery of the materials with which they dealt; because they brought to their perception of new visual surroundings senses cleared of the fog of tradition, the wrongness of some of their theoretical attitudes matters far less than does the soundness of the concrete foundation they built for the new representational control of the visible world.

Two innovations stand to their credit. By reducing the plastic unit to the most elementary shapes, to a geometrical simplicity, and to a few basic colors, they reestablished the genuine construction elements of space architecture on the picture-plane. By their use of the diagonal axis, contradicting the accepted horizontal-vertical space ordering, they revealed a powerful device for creating dynamic spatial experience.

The basic shapes facilitated the juxtaposition of one shape against the other and thus openly manifested the strains and stresses of the experience interrelating them. Because the diagonal axis is in contradiction with one main direction of space, each shape in diagonal position tends to revolve toward the main lines of visual organization—the horizontal vertical axis—thus heightening the dynamic tension.

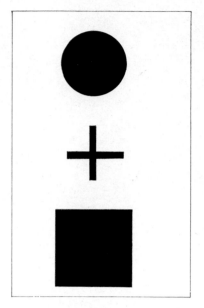

Kasimir Malevich, *Suprematist Elements*

El Lissitzky, *Composition*

Courtesy of Art of This Century

110

Kasimir Malevich, *Suprematist Composition*

Courtesy of Art of This Century

a design students' guide
to the New York World's Fair
compiled for
P/M magazine . . . by Laboratory School
of Industrial Design

The research in movements, stresses, and tensions on the picture surface have had a great influence on the applied arts. Designers of posters and window-display explored the newly discovered idioms and changed their methods from a static symmetry to an elementary dynamic balance.

Paul Rand, *Cover Design*

Joseph Binder, *Poster*

AIR CORPS U.S. ARMY

M. Martin Johnson, *Four Advertising Designs*
Courtesy of Abbott Laboratories

Innovations of spatial expression contributed also to a rejuvenation of typography, for the printed page is also a picture-plane. The mechanical possibilities of the printing process and the rediscovery of elementary plastic relationships were tested in all possible connections.

The space of the printed page came to be consciously considered as a plastic problem. The elements were reduced to their basic geometric shapes. Reduction to essentials is at the borderline of the recognition of object shapes. Every unnecessary detail is eliminated. The spectator's eye is guided with an unmistakable certainty to the essential shapes and their relationships. The interplay of the basic shapes has a strong, dynamic quality based upon the clear plastic relationships of colors, shapes, and lines around the diagonal axis.

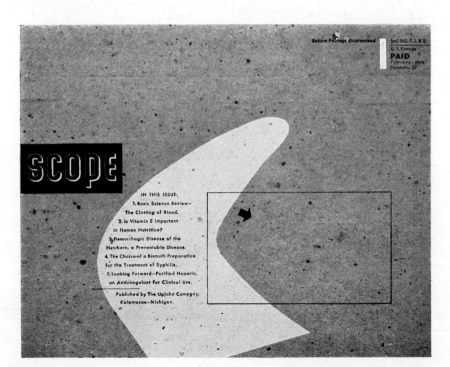

W. Burtin,
Advertising Design

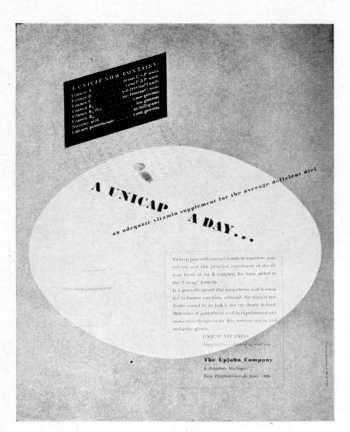

W. Burtin, *Advertising Design*

Taylor Poore, *Poster 1939*

Space construction on the picture surface

The space which the painter tries to encompass is basically the visible order of the events he is experiencing. Painting is a form of thinking. It is, therefore, both natural and inevitable that the steps the painter takes toward formulating spatial experience are conditioned by his ideas and conceptions of the ordering of social existence.

When the expansion into unbounded space, the break with the old frame of reference, had been achieved, the painter turned again to the search for a concrete order. He reached out toward what seemed to him the only positive order in life as he saw it—the order of the machine, the cold precise construction of the engineer. Technological advance, with its precision and economy, seemed the only key to the improvement of social conditions. It appeared that lowering the cost of production would resolve social chaos. The technician was hailed as the prophet of a new social order. And the artist sought to ally himself with the prophet.

 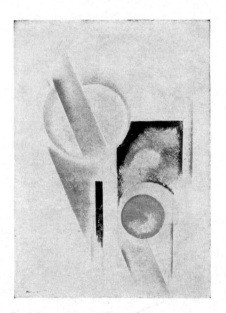 

Rodchenko,
Composition 1918
Courtesy of The Museum of Modern Art

Rodchenko,
Composition 1919

Rodchenko,
Line Construction 1920

Technique was made identical with art, and the art of technique regarded as an independent force of social change. Again the approach was incomplete. One element had been mistaken for the whole.

The painters combined the free-floating and stereometric elements, and welded them into a construction that has its model in the machine. The machine is the fountain of inspiration, not only in its surface qualities and exterior shape but also in its principle of construction. Lines, planes, and forms are combined in a new, dynamic interconnection, transparent and interpenetrable. Mechanical tools, such as the compass and ruler, came into favor as painters struggled to achieve the closest possible similarity to the machine.

Frank Levstik, *Steel Structure.* *Photograph*

L. Moholy Nagy, *Construction in Whites 1928*

The prevailing use of contemporary materials in building, steel frames, glass walls, etc., added further inspiration. The open spans, giving a lightness of construction and allowing a flow of the space within; the new load-and-support relationships, giving a clear insight into the space mechanisms of the building, acted as stimuli. In architecture, there were open, transparent surfaces instead of solid walls; on the picture-plane, likewise, instead of opaque surfaces, there came to be the transparent interpenetration of planes and the open skeletons of lines.

The open network of lines leads out to various directions in space, and a kind of optical cantileverage is achieved—a dynamic space construction.

Ladislav Sutnar. *Advertising Design*

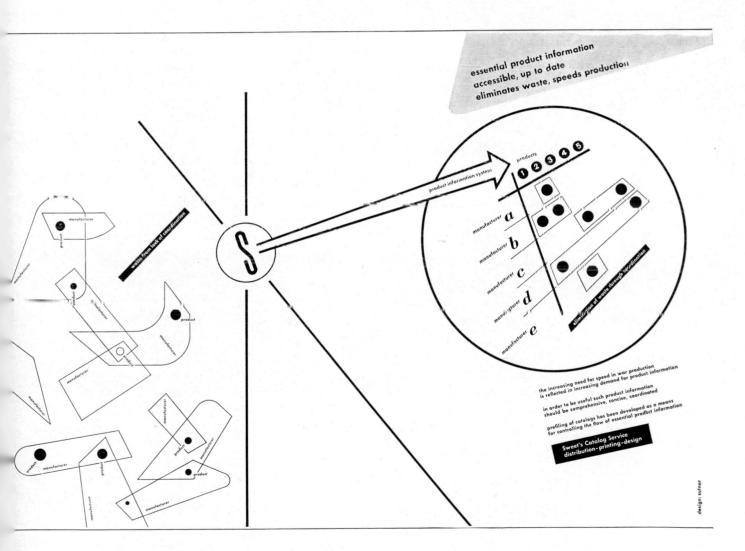

going back to school...

Paul Rand. *Advertising Design*

Conditions in the world the painter lived in cried out for order. Science and technology had advanced; they had totally neglected to domesticate on the social plane the new fields into which they moved. Social ills, domestic and international struggle, unemployment and unused energies, ill-organized days, and finally, a maladjusted individual were the fruits of this neglect.

In this chaotic counterfeit social existence, where almost all materials were misused, including the human being himself, architecture made the first concrete step to build honestly in terms of the present. Pioneer architects recognized that new knowledge demanded a new building principle, that to make use of the scientific understanding of the structural qualities, such as tension, strain, weight, and load; of the new materials, steel, glass, concrete, they must first clear away all debris of inherited styles. Machines and machine production have made the imitation of past styles more and more obsolete. Forty years ago Frank Lloyd Wright said:

> "A structural necessity which shaped Pantheons, monuments, and temples had been reduced by the machine to a skeleton of steel, complete in itself without the artist craftsman touch. . . . The steel frame had been recognized as a legitimate basis for a simple, sincere clothing of plastic material that reveals its essential nature and idealizes its purpose without structural affectation and pretense. The machine smooths away the necessity for the temptation to petty structural deceit, soothes the wearisome struggle to make things seem what they are not and never can be. . . ."

The new discipline of structural honesty has important practical implications. In the best of modern architecture, a building starts, not from the outside—the façade—but from the inside—the ground-plan. The walls articulate this space by dividing and subdividing it. They exclude the outside, giving protection from rain, wind, and sun, but they also model the inside space and the rhythm of the life within. Horizontal and vertical walls are in a clear, functional relationship. The depth of the walls, receding and advancing planes, articulate the space in a dynamic order of living. The result is structural order, an equilibrium of the functioning organism, a living space.

119

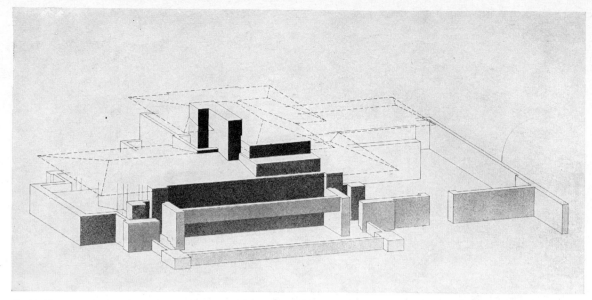

R. B. Tague. *Analysis of the Receding and Advancing Planes of a Frank Lloyd Wright House.*

Living space implies a perpetual balance of opposing directions. The enlarged dimensions of human knowledge demand a new equilibrium between man and nature and individual and society. As Corbusier said: "The individual and the community in that correctly proportioned relationship which is the balance of nature herself—tension between two poles. If there is only one pole the results tend to be zero. Extremes destroy life, for life steers a middle course between extremes. Equilibrium indicates the presence of continuous and unfailing motion. Sleep, stupor, lethargy, and death are not a state of equilibrium. Equilibrium is the point where all forces meet and resolve themselves—poise. Thus can the future town planner read the future destiny of society."

The painter Mondrian, expressed the same understanding in the realm of the plastic arts. He writes:

"Every expression of art has its own laws which accord with the principle law of art and of life: that of equilibrium. On these laws depends the degree of equilibrium that may be realized, and therefore, at what point disequilibrium may be destroyed.

"In Nature, a complete deliverance from tragic feeling is not possible. In life, where the physical form is not only necessary but of the greatest importance, equilibrium will always be very relative. But man, evolving toward the equilibrium of his duality, will create in ever greater degree, in life as in art, equivalent relationships and therefore, equilibrium. Social and economic life today already demonstrate his effort toward an exact equilibrium. Material life will not be forever menaced and made tragic. Nor will our moral life always be oppressed by the domination of material existence."●

This expresses the main current of pioneer contemporary thought in every field of human endeavor; the ardent desire to understand and to order the forces blindly acting today in our life.

● *Piet Mondrian, Pure Plastic Art, 1942*

This thought is order and honesty—in the terms of plastic expression—a perfect equilibrium of the elements—equilibrium identified with the two-dimensional surface itself.

Space is conceived by its control. Extension is expressed by its contraction to the two dimensions. The individual spatial movements of the color planes are measured and expressed by the tension created in pulling them back to the two dimensions. The goal is perfect control, a collective order. No element can live alone. Its life is also that of the two-dimensional whole, which can be only if all the elements are perfectly related and balanced. The picture-plane became like a stretched membrane. Color, shapes, and lines, extending in space toward the top and bottom, laterally, inwards and outwards in depth, effected a precise relationship in which opposing, moving spatial qualities balanced each other on the two-dimensional picture-plane with almost mathematical precision.

The vitality of any equilibrium depends upon the strength of the opposing forces which are in balance. In visual terms, it also depends upon how openly these forces assert themselves. To achieve this maximum of dynamic equilibrium the picture surface was built from basic opposites, rectangular shapes and horizontal and vertical straight lines, blue, red and yellow, pure colors.

"Hence art has to attain an exact equilibrium through the creation of pure plastic means composed in absolute oppositions. In this way, the two oppositions (vertical and horizontal) are in equivalence, that is to say, of the same value: a prime necessity for equilibrium. By means of abstraction, art has interiorized form and color and brought the curved line to its maximum tension: the straight line. Using the rectangular opposition— the constant relationship— establishes the universal individual duality: unity." **Piet Mondrian.**

Piet Mondrian.
Composition
Courtesy of
Art of This Century

Theo Van Doesburg. *Drawing and Typographical Design*

The new ordering principle and the rediscovery of the genuine nature of the two-dimensional picture-plane have had a rejuvenating influence upon painters and upon others. Painters and designers, confronted by the perfect examples of visual rapport and creative discipline, became critical of their own work and began to understand the medium they were manipulating. The crystal-clear formulation of plastic order served as a mirror to show all the wrong conceptions and all the rejections of the honest use of the two-dimensional surface. It helped also to bring out the discrepancy between the genuine nature of the respective materials and their current uses. Typography, product design, and all other fields of optical creation, have gained by the reexamination of the inherent laws of their medium and by the search for better balance.

The painters themselves directed the first steps in this search. Doesburg as early as 1916 applied the findings to typography. His reexamination of the fundamental structural principles of the plastic arts had a far-reaching influence on advertising design and typography. Horizontal and vertical elements in a clear, contrasting relationship lead to a subdivision of the surface with dynamic balance. Symmetrical arrangements of letters and simple rectangular elements blazed the trail for a new typography whose inner spatial logic is dictated by the nature of visual perception with functional emphasis on the message. New type faces were designed, based upon the visual principles discovered by the painters.

Reform in the realm of typography had been sadly needed. Our present form of writing is an incompletely assimilated conglomeration of signs reflecting diverse historical backgrounds and various tools. A harmonious unity between those elements has never been achieved. Capital and lower-case letters never possessed formal unity even in the best classical type-forms. The printed letter is a historical fossil in conformity neither with the laws of visual organization nor with the technological standards of the present, nor with the new psychology of man. Instead of being free to choose its own path in moving about the page, the eye is regimented along a line of print controlled by technically archaic type-standards

Piet Mondrian. *Painting 1932*

Ladislav Sutnar. *Cover Design*

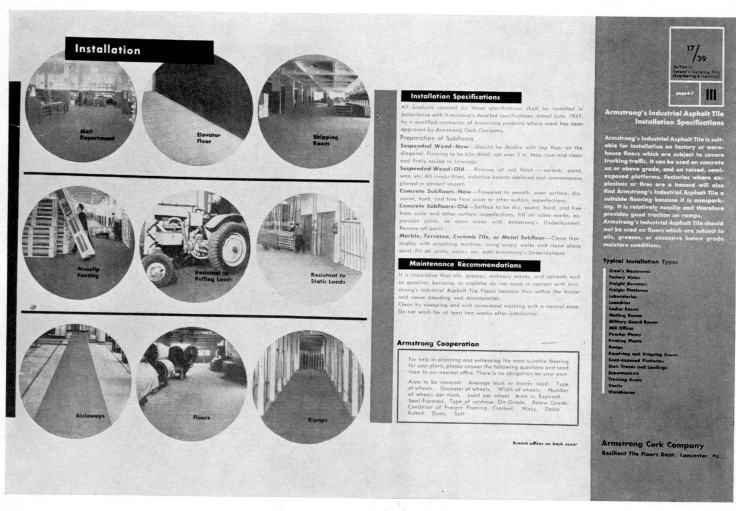

Ladislav Sutnar, *Catalog Design 1942*

Lester Beall. *Advertising Design*

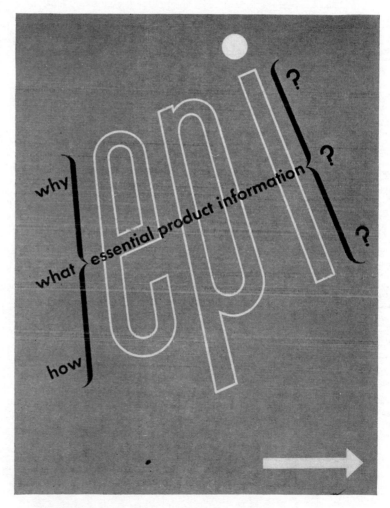

Ladislav Sutnar. *Advertising Design*

The rediscovery of order in terms of plastic experience was conditioned by the social background, by the urgent need of an equilibrium on the socio-economic plane. But this order could be achieved only by a frontal attack of the very basis of the social contradictions. Efforts that avoided open challenge to the causes of the contradictions could achieve only a semi-equilibrium by sacrificing vital aspects of an integral human life. Individual freedom, undisciplined, ran amok as license and brought about a loss of faith in individual qualities. Regimentation, the sacrifice of the individual, became the new social concept of regression and half-measures. This concept anchored itself even in the realm of plastic thought.

To achieve a perfect balance with the two dimensions in the picture, individual plastic qualities were sacrificed. The wealth of the variety of shapes, the richness of colors and values were reduced to stereotyped plastic equations of rectangular shapes. Order became an end in itself instead of a guiding principle. It created its own world—a world of puritan restrictions. This restrained clarity of equilibrium placed rigid restraint upon further ordering. Seeking to eliminate all impurities, it tended to eliminate also many varieties of visual experience.

Clearly needed was the framework of an equilibrium which had room for the individuality of the elements. That equilibrium begins to appear. Doesburg opposed two systems, the horizontal-vertical and the diagonal. Helion began to fill out, step by step, the abstract ground, working with a new variety of the plastic elements, modelling the flat shapes, and twisting and stretching the rectangles into new shapes and binding them into forms.

Theo Van Doesburg.
Composition Arithmetique 1930

126

Jean Helion. *Linoleum Cut*

Jean Helion. *Linoleum Cut 1936*

Innovations in representational idioms caused important progress toward the optical mastery of contemporary space time experiences. But visual communication can only be efficient if it submits itself to the new landscape and the new psychology of contemporary man. And simultaneously with the mastery of the new wider space, visual communication was forced to make some significant adaptations to the contemporary scene.

The number in an audience defines not only the quality and the intensity of the voice of the speaker, but also the nature of speaking. The character of a dialogue is naturally different from that of a speech to a mass meeting. Easel painting, the expression of a historical period, developed a form of visual dialogue. It spoke a language of tête-a-tête. It was the historical manifestation in the pictorial art of the spirit of individualism. But the historical background is changed. The individual dimensions are losing their inflated significance. As points are in a line or lines in a plane, the individual was recognized as irreplaceable only in the terms of the wider dimension. Social interdependence brought up a new meaning of the individual, the social individual. To speak to this new man a different language was required, a language that must penetrate in depth of individual regions but at the same time speak to the largest possible group. This means speaking simultaneously to many. The number of the audience demands an amplification of the sound and a leveling down of the language to common interest and common idioms. The microphone helps to adjust the voice to the greater dimensions of the audience. The mass spectator demands the amplification of optical intensity and a leveling down of the visual language toward common idioms. Such idioms demand simplicity, force, and precision.

"In my search for brilliancy and intensity I made use of the machine as other artists have happened to employ the nude body or still lives. . . . I never amused myself copying a machine. I invent images of machines as others, with their imagination, have invented landscapes. . . . The mechanical element in my work is not a prejudice nor an attitude, but a means of giving a sensation of force and power."•

• *Fernand Leger, Propos d'artistes, 1925*

Simplicity and intensity

Traffic signs, newly important in a world on the move, are the simplest visual statements designed for the mobile observer. They are intense in color, simple in shape, and each one of them clearly constitutes a unit.

Machines, motor cars, streetcars, elevated trains, aeroplanes, flickering-light displays, shop windows, became common features of the contemporary scene. Together with the new richness of light-effects from artificial light sources, the increased dimension of the landscape with the skyscrapers and their intricate inner spatial order above, and the subways underneath, they gave an incomparably greater speed and density to the light stimulations reaching the eye than any previous visual environment had ever presented.

There is no time now for the perception of too many details. The duration of the visual impacts is too short. To attract the eye and convey the full meaning in this visual turmoil of events, the image must possess, like the traffic sign, simplicity of elements and lucid forcefulness.

Precision

Industrial production introduced new objects: machines and machine products, standardized and ready-made units. They were produced with the utmost precision and control dictated by functional needs, utility, and economy. In the confusion of the surrounding object-world these things appeared as the only man-made creations of perfection, coordination, and sense. The mechanical functional clarity of the machine, the perfect harmony of its parts, and the unmistakable rigidity of its inner relationships were an inspiration to men searching for similar qualities in the picture image. Clarity, precision, and economy were compelling values in a world suffocating under the dead weight of undisciplined individualism. Leger says:

"Technique must be more and more exact, the execution must be perfect. . . . I prefer a mediocre painting perfectly executed to a picture, beautiful in intention, but not executed. Nowadays a work of art must bear comparison with any manufactured object. Only the picture, which is an object, can sustain that comparison and challenge time or . . . I deny absolutely the subject and perspective; I introduce the object as a factor reacting on a plastic ensemble."

130

Lester Beall. *Poster*

F. Levstik. *Photograph*

F. Leger. *Painting*
Courtesy of The Museum of Modern Art

Fernand Leger, *Painting*

A. M. Cassandre. *Poster*
Courtesy of The Museum of Modern Art

Light and color

Spatial experience is intimately connected with the experience of light. Without light there is no vision, and without vision there can be no visible space. Space in a visual sense is light-space. Ordinarily this light-space is not apparent to the eye. We perceive spatial relationships only when light is intercepted by some medium. What we actually see as spatial world is the way in which the light is dissected and redirected, that is, modulated by these mediums. The sensory modes of registering the modulated light, the various sensations of color, then, become the means for the spatial ordering of objects and events.

But the experience of light, color means more than sensory data of the spatial world. The word light or color connotes richness, health, and wholeness. Light, thus color, is not merely a spatial sign of the environment; it is a basic human need. In hunger for color is expressed one of man's deepest grasps of reality. "Light, therefore, using the full meaning of the word, transmits energy which is the mainstay of life, and gives to living beings the power of observation; and it is akin to the matter of which all things animate and inanimate are made. The universe is its sphere of action. We do it no more than justice when we speak of the Universe of light."•

Light is the life-giving basic energy for any organic existence. Orientation, in its basic meaning, is man's adaptation of the solar energies bottled up in the infinite variety of nature-forms. The experiencing of light—in other words the sensation of colors—stands for the organism's security and thus has a quality of affirmation. To experience color is to interpret the very core of physical reality in terms of sensory qualities. When one sees colors, unhampered by the notion that they reside in the objects, one's sensory reaction has overtones which originate in one's understanding of light as the basic condition of life. The sensation of color is always, therefore, a symbol of satisfaction of the nervous system.

• *Sir William Bragg, The Universe of Light*

The sources of color experience

Color is an experience—a psychological event. Light and the different distributions of light, by absorption, dispersion and diffraction, are colorless. They become color only as they pass through the structure of the visual receiving set and are registered by the brain. Experiencing color has, then, three basic sources. First is the physical raw material, the radiant energy modulated by the environment. Second are the data supplied directly by the senses. And third are the data furnished by memory, including associations induced by some correspondence between the structure of the current sensory stimulation and previous ones, or by the repeatedly experienced connection between a particular sensory stimulation and an event.

The physical modulation of light

Light may be perceived directly as light-source—the sun, fire, electric light, luminous gas, etc.—colored or shaded by its own intensity.
Light may be modulated on a submicroscopic scale and perceived as constant intrinsic value or color. The white of paper, the green of leaves, the black of velvet—are results of the modulation of the oncoming light by the submicroscopic structure of the respective substances.
Light may be modulated on a grosser scale by the three-dimensional extension of the objects. Then one perceives the sculptured form through modelling by shading.

Light may be modulated and articulated by the various substances, as in the casting of shadows or reflecting, diffusing light; that is, it may be observed as the blocking-out, bleaching, bending of the previously optically latent lightbodies. Then one perceives the space-filling light.

Frank Levstik.
Photograph

Milton Halberstadt, *Photograph*

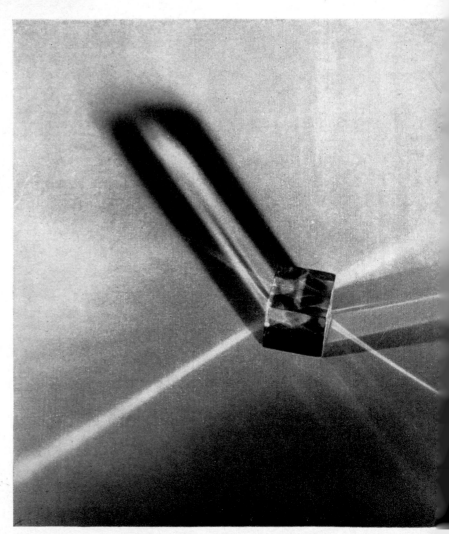

R. B. Tague & W. Keck. *Light Study*
School of Design in Chicago.
Light Workshop

136

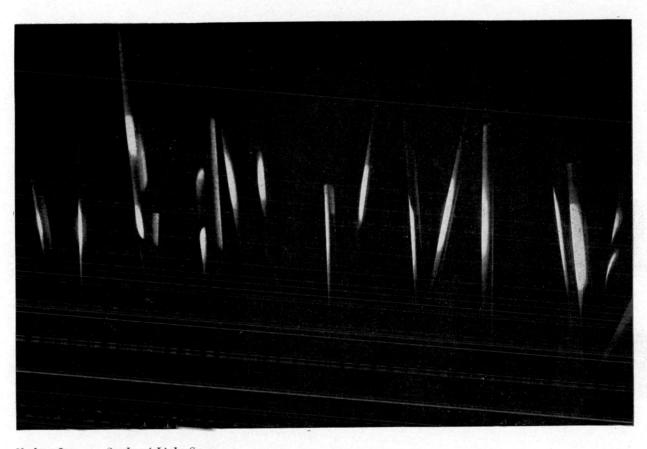

Nathan Lerner. *Study of Light Space*
School of Design in Chicago. Light Workshop

The source of color-sensation in the structure of the sensory receiving set

We distinguish three different qualities of color sensation: hue, or color; brightness, or value; and saturation, or depth. All are based on the physiological evaluation of the physical sources.

Hue, or the actual color, is induced by the differences in wave length of the radiant energies and by the particular structure of the retinal surface upon which these act. This unique interaction of the light agent and the retinal structure gives the foundation of the feeling quality of red, yellow, blue, and so on. The duration of the stimulation plays a decisive role in sensation of hue. Light stimulation must have a certain endurance to induce the sensation of color; short intervals produce only the sensation of brightness.

Brightness, that is, the sensation that one color appears lighter or darker than another, governs the value of the color. It is conditioned partly by the intensity of the stimulation, partly by the neural structure of the retina. The unequal sensitivity of the retina to different wave lengths determines to a great degree which colors appear more luminous or brighter than the others. Yellow, for instance, appears brighter than blue or green.

Saturation is the measure of the actual color content in a given sensation. When we see one red as redder than another, we experience particular sensory quality as manifested in a lesser or greater purity, making the colors more or less rich and full. Red and pink, intense yellow and pale yellow are perceived as different feeling-qualities. The endurance of the stimulation affects the saturation of color. Very long stimulation will reduce the saturation. Too low or too high an intensity tends progressively to eliminate saturation. Furthermore, the structure of the retina modifies saturation. Some colors lose their depth through the stimulation of the periphery of the retinal field.

Dynamic interaction of color sensations

One never registers isolated color sensations. The visual field normally consists of numerous optical qualities and thus color sensations can only be perceived in a dynamic interaction of different types of retinal stimulations. The dynamic interrelations of color sensations are, then, the source of the most important characteristics of color experiences; that is, contrast and spatial value.

Hue, brightness, and saturation of a surface are modified by the adjacent surfaces. The contrast effect is always in the direction of the greatest opposition of colors. If a red and a green surface are juxtaposed on the same picture surface, the red appears redder than it would be if viewed in a color background of closer hue. Similarly, green appears greener when viewed in a yellow, a blue or a brown background. If a grey surface is surrounded by color surface, the grey will assume a tint complementary to the embracing color. If the surrounding color is red, the induced color of grey will be greenish; if the surrounding color is green, the induced color will appear reddish; if blue, yellowish, and so on. The contrast effect will be most powerful when the grey is of a brightness equal to the adjacent color and when this color is highly saturated, that is, when the brightness contrast is reduced to a minimum. The degree of contrast effect is in direct relationship to the nearness of the colors to each other on the picture surface. If the color surfaces are divided with black or color lines, the contrasting result will be diminished in direct proportion to the width of the lines. The contrast result is most thrilling when the saturation of the colors is the greatest. Hues on the blue end of the spectrum manifest a stronger contrast than the colors on the red end of the spectrum.

Color surfaces are modified also in their areas. A light-colored figure on a dark area appears larger than a dark-colored figure of the same size on a light background. A white surface appears to expand most, and a black to contract most. Yellow appears larger than green, blue smaller. Brightness and saturation are important factors in these relative changes. Each brightness-difference amplifies the other's intensity, thus improving the resulting irridation, that is, expansion of the colors.

Goethe observed that the yellowish red seems to "bore into the eye." On the other hand, "just as we like to pursue a pleasant object moving away from us, so we like to look at blue, not because it is pressing in upon us, but because it draws us after it." An eye constructed to bring red light from infinite distance to a focus on the retina can do the same with violet rays from a distance of only two feet. For this and some other intricate physiological reasons, hue, brightness and saturation in their dynamic interrelationship in the visual field are perceived as advancing, receding or circulating, or they appear to be of different weights—falling or floating.

"It is thus seen, that color processes play a double role in the color-space function of vision; they contribute the matter or stuff of the visual field and at the same time determine the way in which the field is organized both bidimensionally and tridimensionally.

Which is to be regarded as primary, color or space, it is too early to decide, but the evidence now at hand points to the increasing recognition of the importance of color for spatial discriminations."●

●Harry Helson, *Problems of Color Constancy, Journal of the Optical Society of America, Vol. 33, No. 10*

The memory source of color experience

The retinal impressions are instantly overlaid by the memory of previous experiences. Blue suggests at once the blue sky; green, the green grasses; white, the white snow. We experience color stimulations primarily with reference to the object world, and consequently color signifies the color of the objects.

This memory overlay also tends to keep the object-color relatively unchanged despite changes of illumination. A white surface, although tinted by the changing atmospheric light to reddish, yellowish, or bluish, is perceived constantly as white.

"Until very recent times the complexion of man was conceived as essentially permanent. At least the strong changes that actually occur in different positions have not been painted until very recent times. A person of fair complexion standing between a green bush and a red brick wall has certainly a face green on one side and red on the other, and if the sun shines on his forehead it may be at times intensely yellow. Still, we are, or at least were, not accustomed to depict these eminently realistic traits. We rather concentrate our attention upon what is permanent in the individual complexion as seen in the ordinary diffused daylight. We are accustomed to see the accidental momentary lights weakened in favour of the permanent impression."● Color appears to reside in the objects entirely independent of illumination.

From the memory also comes another kind of association. Seeing an object means more than placing it in a frame of reference of the three-dimensional world. Even while one is seeing color as substance, one also sees it as cold or warm, bright, gay, sad, depressing, irritating, pleasing, crude, refined, wild, tame, exciting, relaxing, dirty, clean, rich, and possessed of innumerable other feeling qualities. These associations have their origin partly in the neuromuscular process, but partly also in the sum total of the dominant other sensations connected with the color seen. The red of the flower, the blue of the sky, the white of the snow bring back feelings one already has for these things. When one says he sees cold water or a burning red, he is saying that his perception is an intersensory blend, a fusion of two or more sensory experiences.

● *Franz Boas. Primitive Art*

The Game of War. Detail From The Adventures of Kibi
Courtesy of The Museum of Fine Arts, Boston

Value relationships

Man is, as we have seen, primarily object conscious. He measures the surrounding world in terms of things and thus gradually learns to orient himself in his environment. He also learns to evaluate the brightness differences reaching his eye by referring them to objects. As he relates the magnitude of things around him to his own size, and attaches a psychological size and shape constancy to each familiar object, so he endows the objects he knows with color and brightness constancy. The constant color and brightness relationships are serving as an elementary gauge for ordering spatial relationships.

Children's paintings, art works of primitive tribes, Assyrian and Egyptian paintings, early European paintings and those of Eastern Asia, entirely neglect the representation of illumination. They use the value gradation only to segregate one shape from another and thus indicate depth and distance between the things. Brightness values as used by these early painters stood in a clear symbolic role for the object as a whole and were not overloaded with details of minute observation or handicapped by the fixed geometrical system of the illumination perspective. Therefore each shape in its respective value could function forcefully and structurally.

Painting by a Child
Courtesy of The Munson-Williams-Proctor Institute School of Art

Toulouse-Lautrec. *Moulin Rouge*

Courtesy of The Smith College Museum of Art

Lester Beall. *Advertising Design*

Under ordinary conditions, objects in our environment do not receive uniform illumination from every angle. A solid object will receive more light from one side than another, because that side is closer to the light source and thus will intercept the light and cast shadows on the other sides. This variation of tone-values created by uneven illumination is what the eye actually perceives.

The surface of a sphere, a cube, or any other form, gives its own characteristic distribution of light. A spherical surface reflects light in an even flow from light to dark. An angular surface reflects light with sudden contrasts of the light and dark values. Each basic form has a basic light and shadow pattern. An evenly flowing tone-gradation evokes in us a sense of gently curved form. A sudden abrupt change of tone we translate as meaning a sharp or angular surface.

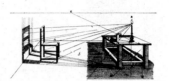

If relatively opaque forms intercept the pathway of light, shadow-bodies are formed. The nature of the light-source, the distance between it and the object, and the angle of the oncoming light rays define the spatial character of the shadow. Thus, the length, the shape, the brightness value of the cast shadow give us additional information about the forms of solids and also indicate the extent and form of the spatial intervals between solids.

Since the discovery of perspective, painters began to represent the optical image of light moulded and bent by the various mediums of the environment. They developed progressive skill first in delineating the three-dimensional sculptural appearance of the object-world, later in mastering light and shadow as space-articulating forces, and finally in representing space as luminous by dissolving solidity into light substance.

In their search for optical fidelity of representation painters were forced to condense more and more the time of observation. They had reduced it almost to infinity. Visual experience, however, is a space-time experience. A distance—an extension in space—has meaning only if a certain time is needed to cover it. The very existence of matter is inseparable from time. It is impossible to conceive a material object as existing instantaneously. The more accurate became the representation of the play of light on the object, therefore, the farther representation departed from a true visual expression of spatial extension. It could never achieve an intimate welding of space-time experience.

Representation went through a development similar to that of the linear perspective. Painters began to chafe against the fetters laid upon space representation by the fixed illumination unity. In breaking these fetters, they achieved the progressive emancipation of the colors and values as plastic forces.

Raphael Santi. *Alba Madonna.* *Courtesy of The National Gallery, Washington, D. C. Mellon Collection.*

Rembrandt. *Portrait of The Artist*
Courtesy of The Metropolitan Museum of Art

Modifications of illumination perspective

Everyday experience with both daylight and artificial illumination leads us, as a rule, to expect the direction of light to be from above. Every shift from this standard light condition is registered and interpreted by us as an exaggeration of spatial dimensions. Lighting from below, from the back, or from one or another unexpected side creates a dynamic spatial effect. The painters exploited this amplification of the illumination perspective. In a similar fashion, as the linear perspective was stretched or condensed to its utmost limits until it reached the greatest dynamic power possible within its limitations, the illumination perspective was bent, moulded, stretched to its utmost. An equivalent to the amplified foreshortening was thus employed in the terms of light and shadow. Instead of a smooth moulding of the forms by gently curved gradation, condensed and stretched value scales were introduced. Another step the painters made corresponded to the device of simultaneous perspective. Corresponding to the simultaneous use of a number of vanishing points and several horizons, they employed in one picture multiple contradictory illumination perspectives. They modified and adapted the distribution of values to the demands of the picture-plane.

The light- and shadow-effects in a representational image imply an abstraction. They are from a fixed point of view, and they indicate the arresting of the position of the spectator, the light-source and the position of the object. But light-and-shadow relationships are in reality transitory, accidental and illusory. The representation of an object under such fixed illumination means its arrest in time, and is consequently a very limited aspect of spatial events. The cubist painters became aware of this contradiction. They recognized that the total disappearance of illumination, or the perfectly even illumination of the surfaces of an object, would make that object inarticulate; would, in effect, cause it to vanish. But they recognized also that brightness relationship is not quite the same as illumination-effect. The arbitrary control of light and shadow can explain the object without arresting it in time. The painter, therefore, devised a graphic metod of fusing the foreground and background by means of an arbitrary extension of light and shade. By subtly graded and consciously controlled values, planes are made to tilt forward or backward without ultimately defining the volume, so that the forms appear to dissolve in the background space. These small shadow-facets are like dynamic direction-signs, guiding the eye to all possible extension in space. It is possible, however, to decompose the solid in such a way that the onlooker can find no spatial unity in terms of the illusory modelling by shading. Spatial unity can then only be accomplished by creating a living spatial-tension between the virtual movements of the advancing and receding values. Striving to find order, one keeps the centrifugal forces of tone values in spatial balance as if suspended by invisible forces. Each brightness value has a clear structural meaning in the organization of this space.

Exactly the same thing happened as had taken place when these same painters broke with linear perspective. Liberated from the fetters of the absolute perspective and modelling by shading, brightness values revealed an intrinsic power of creating spatial experiences on the picture surface without suggesting the three-dimensional object-world. Value gradations, in sharp or blurred definitions, were recognized as genuine plastic forces, and the picture surface achieved a structural clarity and a new sensuous intensity.

Picasso. *Pierrot.* *Courtesy of The Guggenheim Museum of Non-Objective Art*

Influence of photography

While the painters were working toward the breaking up of the representation-habit of modelling by shading, photography reached a hitherto un dreamed of perfection in rendering visible forms by light and shadow.

Photographic representation brought into focus things and events in their actual appearances, revealing much hitherto unnoticed or blurred in our observation. For the first time, men were able to freeze the moving processes of nature into light-and-shadow patterns. What the eye was never able to do, the optical system of the camera and the photo-sensitive emulsion could do. It could record with objectivity and precision the infinite variety of brightness differences reflected from surfaces.

This advance in photographic recording made certain revaluations necessary in visual habits. By its very mechanical perfection it made obsolete the pursuit of the painter's inherited goal: representation of the illusory appearances of familiar things. The more precise the photographic recording, however, the more obvious became the inherent limitation of an absolute perspective. One form can intercept the light and cast a shadow on another in such a way that the spatial character of the object in shadow will be unintelligible. Photography within its own sphere was struggling to find a solution for this problem by unchaining the light-sources and arbitrarily organizing the distribution of light and shadow. The best photographers succeeded in attaining a pliant plastic treatment of light and shadows.

Sharpness and lack of definition

Objects seen from a distance become gradually blurred and indefinite. The Renaissance artists had observed this and introduced it as a device of representation. Through their work it became a stereotyped statement. Photography, however, invalidated in many respects these accepted standards of aerial perspective, just as it had invalidated those of linear perspective.

The eye is an optical instrument so constructed that it can focus only on one plane. We are not able to see near and distant objects sharply at the same time. We never realized this fully until another optical instrument, the camera, brought it forcibly to our attention by freezing the relationship of blurred and clear images on the picture surface of a photograph. Then, we could both see and study an image in all its subtleties of tone modulation. We became sensitive to the spatial significance of sharpness and lack of definition.

Space representation was broadened by this new plastic idiom. Painters found that the principles thus uncovered could be used in visual creation regardless of whether or not there was actual object-representation, for their power lies in ability to give a legitimate space-experience rather than any function of helping the eye in the recognition of objects.

148

Claude Lorrain. *Landscape*

Courtesy of The Cleveland Museum of Art

L. Moholy Nagy. *Marseille Pattern 1929*

Texture Contrast •

Texture

Technological progress contributed greatly to the introduction of another visual idiom: texture. A wider knowledge and more extensive use of materials and structures, the discovery of synthetic materials, and machine culture with its new wealth of surfaces, made familiarity with the new landscape imperative. The unaided eye could not follow, no manual skill could have the precision of coordination to represent, all the intricate surface-qualities of the new man-made materials and objects—a gramophone record with its innumerable variety of sound tracks, for example, or a polished machine-made metal object with its perfect surface quality. Only the camera could cope adequately with the visual domestication of the new wealth of the object-world. Only the camera could keep pace with the speedily unfolding visual properties of the newly created forms and structures.

Photography did more, however, than quicken sensibilities to the texture wealth of the environment. Two points of one or two objects, if close enough together, will be fused as one when they are beyond the visual threshold of discrimination. Photography gave a new, broader meaning to this phenomenon. Explorations with macro-, micro-, and aerial photography opened up visual fields hitherto beyond human reach. In ordinary visual observation, the scale of things is clear in reference to the spectator. Manual representation had traditionally been based also upon a scale related to the spectator. The photographic image, however, is cut out from the familiar spatial frame of reference and there is frequently no cue for deciphering the spatial scale. A micro-photo and an aerial-photo can be easily confused. Space is condensed or expanded according to the optical accessories used in its recording.

• *Work done for the author's course in Visual Fundamentals.*

Because of the relativity of the spatial scale the varied qualities of texture values had become the only visible signs able to indicate spatial relationships. Form modelled by shading could no longer be regarded as the sole space-ordering agent of brightness-value differences. Visual form became only a borderline case in a new, more extensive visual context—texture surface.

Walter Peterhans. *Ophelia—Homage to Rimbaud*

Following the pioneer photographers, painters began to assimilate in the picture-image texture qualities inherent in every material. This new sensory property enriched the image. For texture has a unique dimension. The particular rhythm of light and dark that makes up visible texture is beyond our ability to distinguish in any form of visual organization in terms of modelling by shading. It has a fine grain of sensory impact which can be comprehended only in its structural correspondence to other sensory feelings. The surface-texture of grass, concrete, metal, burlap, silk, newspaper, or fur, strongly suggestive of the qualities of touch, we experience visually in a kind of intersensory blend. We see, not light and dark, but qualities of softness, coldness, roughness, restfulness—sight and touch are fused into a single whole.

Henry Kann
Exercise with Transparent Planes
School of Design in Chicago
R. B. Tague, Instructor

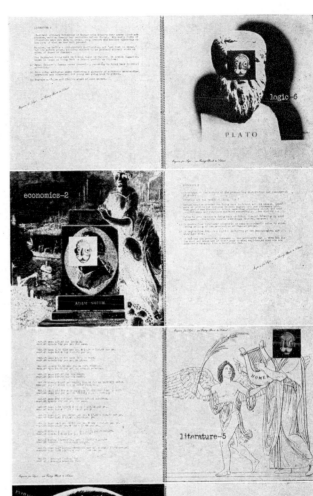

Paul Rand. *Advertising Design*

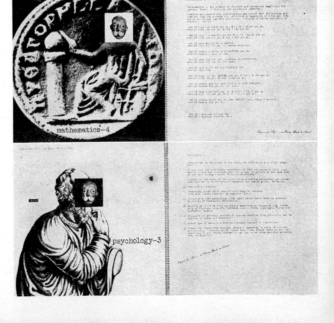

153

Influence of artificial light-sources

Contemporary man lives in a city environment which offers through each artificial light source an optical scene at night incomparable to any previous visual experience. Buildings that were modelled under the sun into a clear sculptural form, under the simultaneously acting artificial light-sources lose their three-dimensional quality. Contours are obscured. The light spots, coming from inside and outside simultaneously, and the fusion of luminosity and chiaroscuro, break up the solid form as the measuring unit of space. The fluctuating, vibrating light-patterns cannot be fitted together into an optically modelled form. A spatial interpretation can be achieved only by assuming a more dynamic spatial unity than the illusory forms sculptured by light and shadow. Brightness differences, the sharp or the blurred definitions, the texture of light span the space by their intrinsic advancing—or receding—values. Here also was a strong environmental influence forcing the painter to reconsider and discard his old habit of modelling by shading.

Artificial lighting not only introduced a new approach to spatial representation but contributed to a broadening and a redirection of visual experiences and consequently to a radical readjustment of man's visual sensibilities.

"With our present methods of producing tremendous brightnesses within very small areas, and controlling these almost completely both as to intensity and as to spatial position, man's triumph overnight has been rendered practically complete. At the same time a whole new field of investigation has separated itself out from the traditional optics, *viz.*, that of illumination engineering, a study which stands in closest relation to physiological and psychological optics. Leading illumination engineers are now willing to recognize that their science can no longer be considered as simply a branch of applied physics, as was the case in the days when it was believed that the determination of photometric values exhausted the problems of the field. It is realized now that a study of the effects of light on the human organism is equally important, so important, in fact, as to constitute a separate branch of illumination engineering."●

● *David Katz, The Word of Color, London, 1935*

154

Bernice Abbott. *Night View*

R. J. Wolff. *Painting 1937*
Courtesy of T. B. Foley

Gyorgy Kepes. *Experiment With Light 1940*

R. J. Wolff. *Construction in Light 1938*

"The chief motivation behind this work lies in the new indoor environment which has been created by contemporary architecture. The so-called free arts can no longer ignore the physiological factors that have made the framed picture and the pedestaled object as architecturally disturbing as the paneled ~ll and the chandelier.
"The Construction in Light is an attempt to create images out of actual light and space. Form achieves identity without materiality. The techniques of painting, sculpture and light are combined to serve architectonic ends, as well as a medium of free expression." Robert J. Wolff.

L. Moholy Nagy. *Photogram 1923*

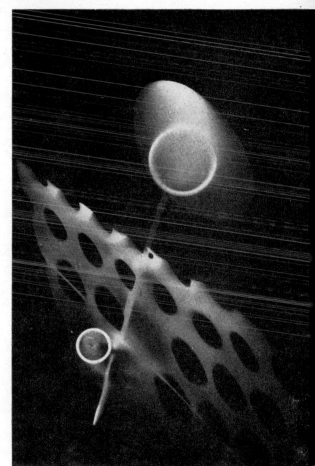

157

Man Ray. *Rayograph 1922*
Courtesy of The Museum of Modern Art

L. Moholy Nagy. *Photogram 1939*

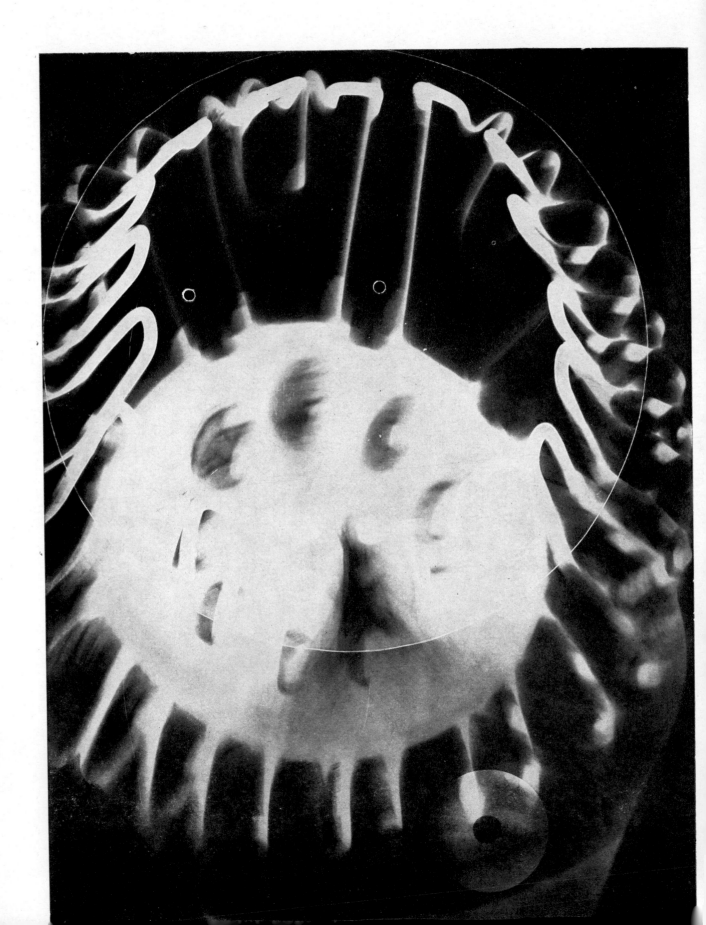

N. Lerner. *Study of Light Volume 1939*
Light Workshop, School of Design in Chicago

Photographers, painters, and other experimenters with light are important pioneers in testing the psycho-physiological effects of plastic organization of light. Helmholtz reminded the scientists a long time ago that "A careful study of the paintings of the great masters . . . is of great importance for physiological optics." The study of the expressions of the contemporary masters is no less significant. Not only could they aid research in psychological optics, but help to retrain us to a better understanding of the shaping of our physical environment.

"Brightness exciting stimuli have an effect, not only in the same manner on all sense organs, not only from the sense organs upon the muscles, and vice versa from the muscles upon the eye, but there is induced by such stimuli a modification of the whole organism. . . . My clinical observations also prove that the study of the reactions of the organism to brightness and darkness exciting stimuli is calculated to clear up problems, which have a scope far beyond the psychology of perception and that here we have to do with fundamental biological processes of manifold significance for clinical practice as well."•

• *Walter Barnstein, Journal of General Psychology, 1936*

Lester Beall. *Advertising Design, Photogram*

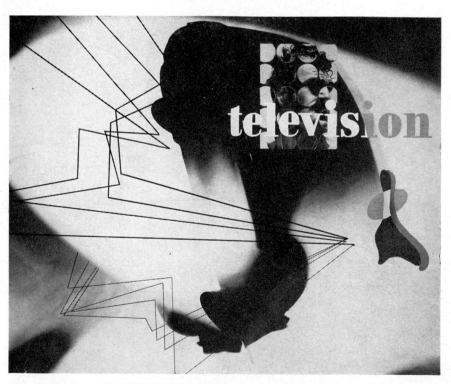

Harold Walter. *Poster With Photogram*

Gyorgy Kepes. *Advertising Design, Photogram 1*

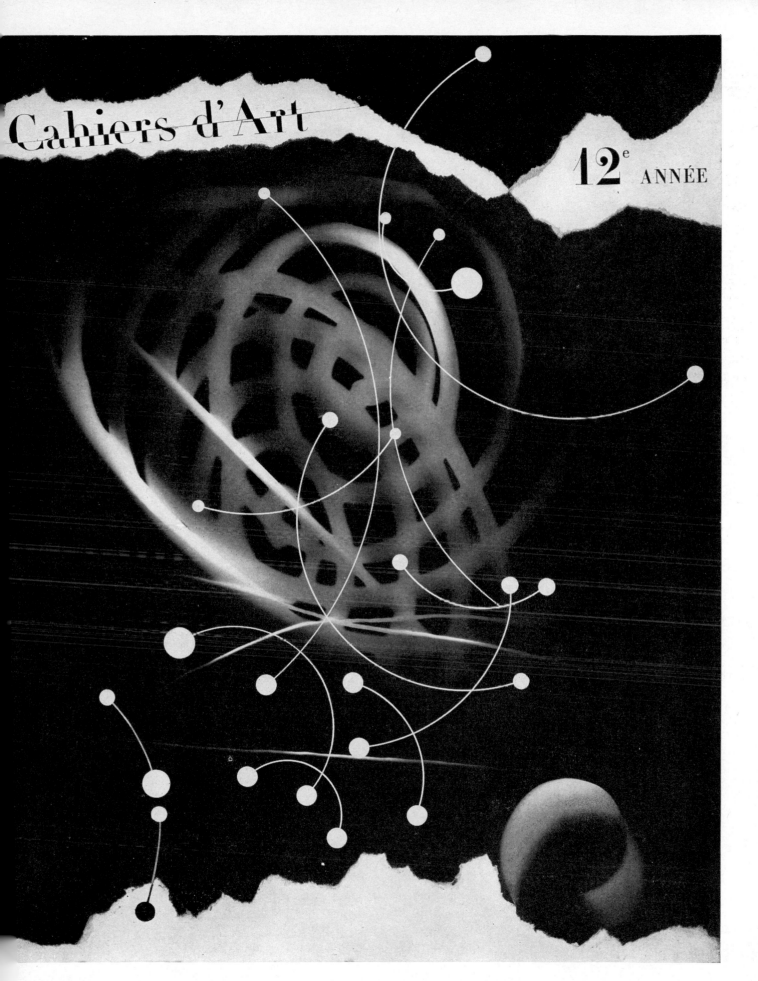

Cahiers d'Art

12e ANNÉE

Representation of the relationship of colors

Early forms of representation invariably showed the local color of the object in spite of changes of illumination, just as they retained the constant brightness value, the actual size and shape of the object, regardless of perspective distortion. In the painting of the Paleolithic man, Assyrian and Egyptian artists, Greek vase painters, early European painters, children and primitives, color stood in a clear symbolic role for the objects as a whole and was not overloaded with details of minute observations. The color-areas were not handicapped in their elementary sensory qualities.

The more precise the observation of the appearance of the object and the sharper man's ability to distinguish optical effects, the less the color-areas on the picture surface could function in full sensory intensity. Just as the size and form of the object were altered by linear perspective, so the local color lost its absolute reference to the object. Since the Renaissance, representational tendencies have been focused upon the exact portrayal of the modification of local colors by the effects of illumination. Light and shadow, the reflection of one color on another, the color of the light-source, and other optical modifications were carefully recorded as painters strove for accurate representation of the optical appearances of objects from one fixed point of view. Unconditional surrender to the appearances of the thing was an inevitable consequence, and through such submission to a shallow naturalism, the sensory quality of the colors was gradually drained out.

It is a familiar experience that the sensory quality innate in a sign, in a word, in an event, comes in time to be absorbed by the thing for which it stands. Only by repeating a familiar word over and over again, for instance, can one bring back into it the sensory quality of its sound, make it independent of context, and restore its original sensory intensity. One must look at a familiar landscape from a position which gives an unfamiliar retinal image of the familiar relationships of its component objects if one is to sense the original intensity of the colors of that landscape. Only then will the colors, before embedded in their objects, be set free to speak in their own pure language, the language of the senses. The consistent search to represent all apparent aspects of the visible surroundings led, paradoxically, to the liberation of the sensory quality of color. In the control of the play of light on objects, painters had included the space between the objects in the object-world. They had widened the representational grasp of objects by including the atmosphere, the air, as a light-modulating substance. They were trying to represent with pigment the space-filling light.

164

T. M. W. Turner. *Burning of The Houses of Parliament, 1834*
Courtesy of The Cleveland Museum of Art

Georges Seurat.

Detail of
Sunday on The Grand Jatte 1884-86
Courtesy of The Art Institute of Chicago

This attempt to find an adequate articulation of reflected light on pigments that could match the living, vibrating, sensory richness of the transmitted atmospheric light—the new subject matter—led ultimately to a new basis of representation. The painters scientifically discovered the laws of color mixing. They realized that they could not represent the luminosity of the transmitted light of atmosphere by mixing colors in the ordinary way, by the subtractive pigment mixing. In the scientific researches of Chevreul and Helmholtz they found their answer: color could be mixed on the retina. The device they invented to create this optical mixture of color light on the retina was the breaking up of the previously smoothly modelled color surface into small color dots or lines. These were combined in an order that fused them on the retina into a luminous quality. This innovation opened the road in two directions. One was the rediscovery of the color plane as the basic building element of the plastic image—in its embryonic form a color spot of the impressionist paintings. The other was the conscious application of the additive color mixing which made it clear that the image is man-made, that the human factor is an integer element in the image, and that representation of spatial experiences cannot be the facsimile of the spatial reality, but must be a corresponding structure based upon the human receiving set.

The actual result in painting, meanwhile, was in most cases merely a short-hand record of vibrating color effect. Visual experience was formulated only in terms of the eye as a physiological apparatus, and the picture was simply a replica of the color dots on the retina blown up in the scale of the picture-plane. Here plastic organization reached the zero point.

165

Picasso. *Pierrot*

Henri Matisse. *Harmony in Yellow*
Reproduction Courtesy
The Art Institute of Chicago

The space dimension of color

But here also new directions of plastic organization were inherent. The color spot now lived its own true existence. It could be tested in various functions on the picture surface. Dissociated from fixed illumination, the color surfaces manifested first of all their intrinsic spatial value. This inherent space dimension of color was controlled and explored for building solids on the surface. After long aberrations when color was used only as coloring, and indicated the color of an object, color now constituted the object. The weight and the bulk of the mass were modelled from and by the advancing and receding colors. Forms could now grow from colors, and the structural use of color be made to give a sense of spatial reality that no previous representational method had achieved. To make the colors work in this structural sense it is necessary to understand all their spatial actions. The interest of the painters since impressionism has been concentrated on the testing of colors in their advancing, receding, expanding, and contracting actions.

New significance now attached to the fact that colors are perceived on the picture surface in a dynamic interaction with one another, so that each color quality has only a relative value, because it undergoes modifications due to its interrelationship with other color surfaces. This research necessarily included learning how one color modifies the other by being placed next to it. It sought also knowledge of active and passive characteristics—when and how one color arrests the eye with a greater power than another. The more knowledge he acquired, the bolder the painter became in dissociating the color surfaces from the object-belonging. The color dots of the impressionist painters, through the color facets of Cezanne; the decorative color pattern of Gauguin and Matisse, reached full growth in the work of the cubist and attained a final purity and power in the work of Malevitch and Mondrian.

166

The feeling dimensions of color

The emancipation of the color spot from slavish subordination to the object and fixed illumination brought another important result. It gave painters the initial impetus to go beyond the frontiers of another tradition of color-expression.

It was pointed out previously that through an intricate interaction of the structure of the sensory receiving set and memory factors, color sensations are endowed with unique feeling qualities. We are able to see, or it appears that we are able to see, what the eye structurally is not capable of seeing. We see warm and cold, quiet and loud, sharp and dull, light and heavy, sad and gay, static and dynamic, wild and tame colors. On the other hand, we have acoustical and olfactory sensations that have colors, brightness, saturation and spatial qualities of height, width, length, weight, direction, and movement.

There is a common structural basis of all kinds of sensations. We have a faculty of perceiving structural qualities common in sight, hearing, touch, and taste. Sight and hearing particularly show and inexhaustible reservoir of interchangeable structure of sensations. The sensations may call forth intensive emotional response, without rising into consciousness. Painters, musicians, poets, and scientists, aware of the significance and creative potentialities inherent in this structural correspondence, searched and worked for a creative control, for a synchronization of the senses. Goethe made important contributions. A. W. Schlegel, the German romanticist of the early nineteenth century, invented a scale of colors corresponding to human vowels, and he attributed a special significance to every particular conjunction of the vowel color. "A" represents the light clear red, and signifies youth, friendship, radiance. "I" stands for celestial blue, symbolizing love. "O" is purple, "V" stands for violet, etc. Recent scientific research offered new important data. Von Hornbostal made extensive study of the common factor of the different sensory data. He states his finding in one of the experiments as follows: "To a particular smell, say benzol, the correspondingly bright gray is chosen on the color disc, and to the same smell, from the series of tuning forks, the correspondingly bright tone." Franz Boas brings observations from another field. He writes:

"Most of us will feel that a high pitch and exaggerated length, perhaps also the vowel i (English ee) indicate smallness, while low pitch and length and the vowels a, o, u (English oo) indicate large size. . . Large or small size, or intensity may be expressed by variations of sound. Thus Nez Perce, an Indian language spoken in Idaho, changes n to l to indicate smallness; Dakota has many words in which s changes to sh, or z to j, indicating greater intensity. . . Undoubtedly the particular kind of synesthesia between sound, sight and touch has played its role in the growth of language."•

• Franz Boas, General Anthropology, 1938

In the traditional representation these intersensory qualities of colors were fastened to the objects, in the same way as the intrinsic spatial values of brightness and hue were embedded in the objects and thus hampered by linear perspective and modelling by shading. Contemporary painters broke these old ties. Colors taken from the object context may call forth emotional responses coming deeper than from the conscious state. Painters employing these intersensory qualities of color were able to arouse emotional reactions of a great intensity and variety. This approach had a great rejuvenating influence. The expressionist painters in search of a color structure which could induce strong emotional responses went boldly ahead and moulded colors and shapes in a hitherto undared flexibility.

It is interesting to note that this approach was in its first steps the psychological equivalent of the perspective vision that approaches the visible world from a fixed point of view. The fixed point of view, in this last phase of individualism, was psychological. One saw what he was able to see from his psychological position. As linear perspective distorted, shaped, and modified actual spatial characteristics according to a particular angle of vision, so the psychological equivalent of linear perspective distorted, modelled, and modified color appearance and color characteristics of objects according to the individual's current attitude, emotion, wishes, desires; the angle of psychological vision. The consistent development in this subjective treatment of color appearance of things led to a negation of color as fixed objective reality, just as the consistent search for the representation of perspective appearance had led to the negation of the perspective-idea, the fixed optical reality. But after an utterly subjective appraisal of the early expressionist painters, painting a face blue, red, or yellow, and an animal green, black, or any other color which is not its natural color, but is what one may call a psychological angle of vision, the object-content falls out entirely. Color remains as a universal keyboard of feelings. Color representation reaches a higher level of objectivity. And once more, disintegration opened the way for fuller integration. Color was regained as a basic material of plastic creation, a spatial element that can be organized structurally as well as used as an elementary sensory quality with an emotional effect on the beholder.

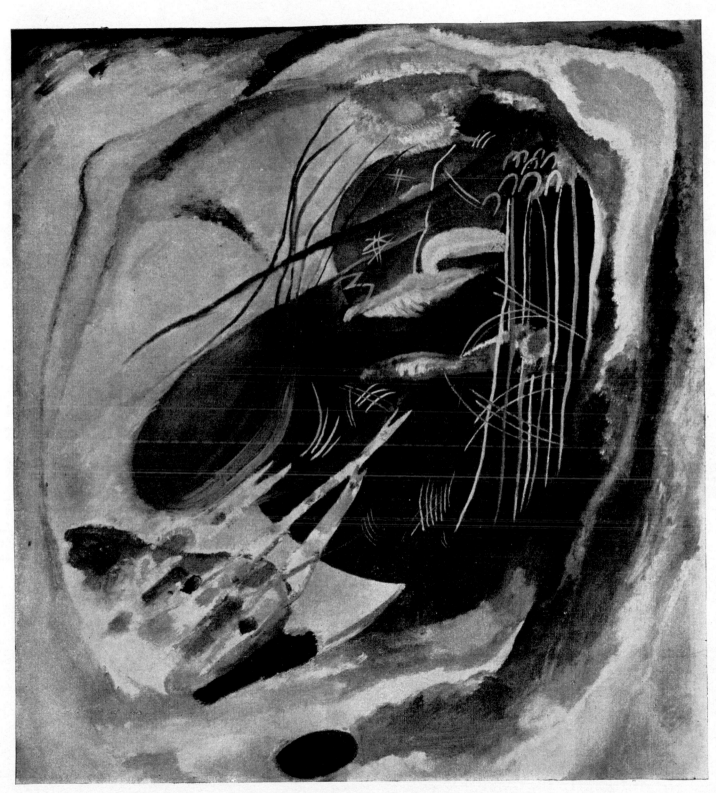

W. Kandinsky. *Picture With Three Spots.* Courtesy of The Guggenheim Museum of Non-Objective Art

Representation of movement

Matter, the physical basis of all spatial experience and thus the source material of representation, is kinetic in its very essence. From atomic happenings to cosmic actions, all elements in nature are in perpetual interaction—in a flux complete. We are living a mobile existence. The earth is rotating; the sun is moving; trees are growing; flowers are opening and closing; clouds are merging, dissolving, coming and going; light and shadow are hunting each other in an indefatigable play; forms are appearing and disappearing; and man, who is experiencing all this, is himself subject to all kinetic change. The perception of physical reality cannot escape the quality of movement. The very understanding of spatial facts, the meaning of extension or distances, involves the notion of time—a fusion of space-time which is movement. "Nobody has ever noticed a place except at a time or a time except at a place," said Minkowsky in his *Principles of Relativity*.

The sources of movement perception

As in a wild jungle one cuts new paths in order to progress further, man builds roads of perception on which he is able to approach the mobile world, to discover order in its relationships. To build these avenues of perceptual grasp he relies on certain natural factors. One is the nature of the retina, the sensitive surface on which the mobile panorama is projected. The second is the sense of movement of his body—the kinesthetic sensations of his eye muscles, limbs, head, which have a direct correspondence with the happenings around him. The third is the memory association of past experience, visual and non-visual; his knowledge about the laws of the physical nature of the surrounding object-world.

The shift of the retinal image

We perceive any successive stimulation of the retinal receptors as movement, because such progressive stimulations are in dynamic interaction with fixed stimulations, and therefore the two different types of stimulation can be perceived in a unified whole only as a dynamic process, movement. If the retina is stimulated with stationary impacts that follow one another in rapid succession, the same sensation of optical movement is induced. Advertising displays with their rapidly flashing electric bulbs are perceived in continuity through the persistence of vision and therefore produce the sensation of movement, although the spatial position of the light bulbs is stationary. The movement in the motion picture is based upon the same source of the visual perception.

The changes of any optical data indicating spatial relationships, such as size, shape, direction, interval, brightness, clearness, color, imply motion. If the retinal image of any of these signs undergoes continuous regular change, expansion or contraction, progression or graduation, one perceives an approaching or receding, expanding or contracting movement. If one sees a growing or disappearing distance between these signs, he perceives a horizontal or vertical movement.

"Suppose for instance, that a person is standing still in a thick woods, where it is impossible for him to distinguish, except vaguely and roughly in a mass of foliage and branches all around him, what belongs to one tree and what to another, and how far the trees are separated. The moment he begins to move forward, however, everything disentangles itself and immediately he gets an apperception of the content of the woods and the relationships of objects to each other in space."●

From a moving train, the closer the object the faster it seems to move. A far-away object moves slowly and one very remote appears to be stationary. The same phenomenon, with a lower relative velocity, may be noticed in walking, and with a still higher velocity in a landing aeroplane or in a moving elevator.

The role of relative velocity

The velocity of motion has an important conditioning effect. Motion can be too fast or too slow to be perceived as such by our limited sensory receiving set. The growth of trees or of man, the opening of flowers, the evaporation of water are movements beyond the threshold of ordinary visual grasp. One does not see the movement of the hand of a watch, of a ship on a distant horizon. An aeroplane in the highest sky seems to hang motionless. No one can see the traveling of light as such. In certain less rapid motions beyond the visual grasp, one is able, however, to observe the optical transformation of movement into the illusion of a solid. A rapidly whirled torch loses its characteristic physical extension, but it submerges into another three-dimensional-appearing solid—into the virtual volume of a cone or a sphere. Our inability to distinguish sharply beyond a certain interval of optical impacts makes the visual impressions a blur which serves as a bridge to a new optical form. The degree of velocity of its movement will determine the apparent density of that new form. The optical density of the visible world is in a great degree conditioned by our visual ability, which has its particular limitations.

The kinesthetic sensation

When a moving object comes into the visual field, one pursues it by a corresponding movement of his eyes, keeping it in a stationary or nearly stationary position on the retina. Retinal stimulation, then, cannot alone account for the sensation of movement. Movement-experience, which is undeniably present in such a case, is induced by the sensation of muscle movements. Each individual muscle-fibre contains a nerve end, which registers every movement the muscle makes. That we are able to sense space in the dark, evaluate direction-distances in the absence of contacted bodies, is due to this muscular sensation—the kinesthetic sensation.

● Helmholtz, Physiological Optics

E. G. Lukacs. *Action*
From Herbert Bayer Design Class

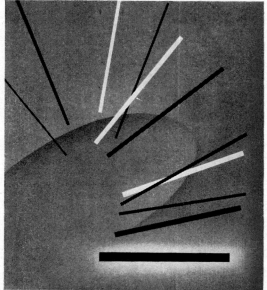

H. L. Carpenter. *Movement* •

• *Work done for the author's course in Visual Fundamentals.*

Paul Rand. *Cover Design*

Memory sources

Experience teaches man to distinguish things and to evaluate their physical properties. He knows that bodies have weight; unsupported they will of necessity fall. When, therefore, he sees in midair a body he knows to be heavy, he automatically associates the direction and velocity of its downward course. One is also accustomed to seeing small objects as more mobile than large ones. A man is more mobile than a mountain; a bird is more frequently in motion than a tree, the sky, or other visible units in its background. Everything that one experiences is perceived in a polar unity in which one pole is accepted as a stationary background and the other as a mobile, changing figure.

Traditional representational devices

Through all history painters have tried to suggest movement on the stationary picture surface, to translate some of the optical signs of movement-experience into terms of the picture-image. Their efforts, however, have been isolated attempts in which one or the other sources of movement-experience were drawn upon; the shift of the retinal image, the kinesthetic experience, or the memory of past experiences were suggested in two-dimensional terms.

These attempts were conditioned mainly by the habit of using things as the basic measuring unit for every event in nature. The constant characteristics of the things and objects, first of all the human body, animals, sun, moon, clouds, or trees, were used as the first fixed points of reference in seeking relationships in the optical turmoil of happenings.

Therefore, painters tried first to represent motion by suggesting the visible modifications of objects in movement. They knew the visual characteristics of stationary objects and therefore every observable change served to suggest movement. The prehistoric artist knew his animals, knew, for example, how many legs they had. But when he saw an animal in really speedy movement, he could not escape seeing the visual modification of the known spatial characteristics. The painter of the Altamiro caves who pictures a running reindeer with numerous legs, or the twentieth century cartoonist picturing a moving face with many superimposed profiles, is stating a relationship between what he knows and what he sees.

Ch. D. Gibson.
The Gentleman's Dilemma cc. 1900

Other painters, seeking to indicate movement, utilized the expressive distortion of the moving bodies. Michaelangelo, Goya, and also Tintoretto, by elongating and stretching the figure, showed distortion of the face under the expression of strains of action and mobilized numerous other psychological references to suggest action.

The smallest movement is more possessive of the attention than the greatest wealth of relatively stationary objects. Painters of many different periods observed this well and explored it creatively. The optical vitality of the moving units they emphasized by dynamic outlines, by a vehement interplay of vigorous contrast of light and dark, and by extreme contrast of colors. In various paintings of Tintoretto, Maffei, Veronese, and Goya, the optical wealth and intensity of the moving figures are juxtaposed against the submissive, neutral, visual pattern of the stationary background.

Harunobu. *Windy Day Under Willow*
Courtesy of The Art Institute of Chicago

Maffei. *Painting*

The creative exploitation of the successive stimulations of the retinal receptors in terms of the picture surface was another device many painters found useful. Linear continuance arrests the attention and forces the eye into a pursuit movement. The eye, following the line, acts as if it were on the path of a moving thing and attributes to the line the quality of movement. When the Greek sculptors organized the drapery of their figures which they represented in motion, the lines were conceived as optical forces making the eye pursue their direction.

We know that a heavy object in a background that does not offer substantial resistance will fall. Seeing such an object we interpret it as action. We make a kind of psychological qualification. Every object seen and interpreted in a frame of reference of gravitation is endowed with potential action and could appear as falling, rolling, moving. Because we customarily assume an identity between the horizontal and vertical directions on the picture surface and the main directions of space as we perceive them in our everyday experiences, every placing of an object representation on the picture surface which contradicts the center of gravity, the main direction of space—the horizontal or vertical axis—causes that object to appear to be in action. Top and bottom of the picture surface have a significance in this respect.

G. McVicker. *Study of Linear Movement*

*Work done for the author's course
in Visual Fundamentals*

*Sponsored by The Art Director's Club
of Chicago. 1938*

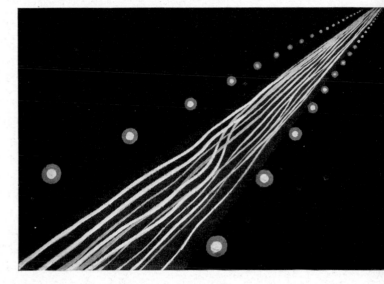

Lee King. *Study of Movement Representation*

*Work done for the author's course
in Visual Fundamentals*

School of Design in Chicago

Contemporary attempts of movement representation

Whereas the visual representation of depth had found various complete systems, such as linear perspective, modelling by shading, a parallel development had never taken place in the visual representation of motion. Possibly this has been because the tempo of life was comparatively slow; therefore, the ordering and representation of events could be compressed without serious repercussions in static formulations. Events were measured by things, static forms identical with themselves, in a perpetual fixity. But this static point of view lost all semblance of validity when daily experiences bombarded man with a velocity of visual impacts in which the fixity of the things, their self-identity, seemed to melt away. The more complex life became, the more dynamic relationships confronted man, in general and in particular, as visual experiences, the more necessary it became to revaluate the old relative conceptions about the fixity of things and to look for a new way of seeing that could interpret man's surroundings in their change. It was no accident that our age made the first serious search for a reformulation of the events in nature into dynamic terms. This reformulation of our ideas about the world included almost all the aspects one perceives. The interpretation of the objective world in the terms of physics, the understanding of the living organism, the reading of the inner movement of social processes, and the visual interpretation of events were, and still are, struggling for a new gauge elastic enough to expand and contract in following the dynamic changes of events.

The influence of the technological conditions

The environment of the man living today has a complexity which cannot be compared with any environment of any previous age. The skyscrapers, the street with its kaleidoscopic vibration of colors, the window-displays with their multiple mirroring images, the street cars and motor cars, produce a dynamic simultaneity of visual impression which cannot be perceived in the terms of inherited visual habits. In this optical turmoil the fixed objects appear utterly insufficient as the measuring tape of the events. The artificial light, the flashing of electric bulbs, and the mobile game of the many new types of light-sources bombard man with kinetic color sensations having a keyboard never before experienced. Man, the spectator, is himself more mobile than ever before. He rides in streetcars, motorcars and aeroplanes and his own motion gives to optical impacts a tempo far beyond the threshold of a clear object-perception. The machine man operates adds its own demand for a new way of seeing. The complicated interactions of its mechanical parts cannot be conceived in a static way; they must be perceived by understanding of their movements. The motion picture, television, and, in a great degree, the radio, require a new thinking, i.e., seeing, that takes into account qualities of change, interpenetration and simultaneity.

Man can face with success this intricate pattern of the optical events only as he can develop a speed in his perception to match the speed of his environment. He can act with confidence only as he learns to orient himself in the new mobile landscape. He needs to be quicker than the event he intends to master. The origin of the word "speed" has a revealing meaning. In original form in most languages, speed is intimately connected with success. Space and speed are, moreover, in some early forms of languages, interchangeable in meaning. Orientation, which is the basis of survival, is guaranteed by the speed of grasping the relationships of the events with which man is confronted.

Social and psychological motivations

Significantly, the contemporary attempts to represent movement were made in the countries where the vitality of living was most handicapped by outworn social conditions. In Italy, technological advances and their economical-social consequences, were tied with the relics of past ideas, institutions. The advocates of change could see no clear, positive direction. Change as they conceived it meant expansion, imperialist power policy. The advance guard of the expanding imperialism identified the past with the monuments of the past, and with the keepers of these monuments; and they tried to break, with an uninhibited vandalism, everything which seemed to them to fetter the progress toward their goals. "We want to free our country from the fetid gangrene of professors, archaeologists, guides and antique shops," proclaimed the futurist manifesto of 1909. The violence of imperialist expansion was identified with vitality; with the flux of life itself. Everything which stood in the way of this desire of the beast to reach his prey was to be destroyed. Movement, speed, velocity became their idols. Destructive mechanical implements, the armoured train, machine gun, a blasting bomb, the aeroplane, the motor car, boxing, were adored symbols of the new virility they sought.

In Russia, where the present was also tied to the past and the people were struggling for the fresh air of action, interest also focused on the dynamic qualities of experience. The basic motivation of reorientation toward a kinetic expression there was quite similar to that of the Italian futurists. It was utter disgust with a present held captive by the past. Russia's painters, writers, like Russia's masses, longed to escape into a future free from the ties of outworn institutions and habits. Museums, grammar, authority, were conceived of as enemies; force, moving masses, moving machines were friends. But this revolt against stagnant traditions, this savage ridiculing of all outworn forms, opened the way for the building of a broader world. The old language, which as Mayakovsky said "was too feeble to catch up with life," was reorganized into kinetic idioms of revolutionary propaganda. The visual language of the past, from whose masters Mayakovsky asked with just scorn, "Painters will you try to capture speedy cavalry with the tiny net of contours?" was infused with new living blood of motion picture vision.

In their search to find an optical projection which conformed to the dynamic reality as they sensed and comprehended it, painters unconsciously repeated the path traced by advancing physical science.

Their first step was to represent on the same picture-plane a sequence of positions of a moving body. This was basically nothing but a cataloging of stationary spatial locations. The idea corresponded to the concept of classical physics, which describes objects existing in three-dimensional space and changing locations in sequence of absolute time. The concept of the object was kept. The sequence of events frozen on the picture-plane only amplified the contradiction between the dynamic reality and the fixity of the three-dimensional object-concept.

Their second step was to fuse the different positions of the object by filling out the pathway of their movement. Objects were no longer considered as isolated, fixed units. Potential and kinetic energies were included as optical characteristics. The object was regarded to be either in active motion, indicating its direction by "lines of force." or in potential motion, pregnant with lines of force, which pointed the direction in which the object would go if freed. The painters thus sought to picture the mechanical point of view of nature, devising optical equivalents for mass, force, and gravitation. This innovation signified important progress, because the indicated lines of forces could function as the plastic forces of two-dimensional picture-plane.

The third step was guided by desire to integrate the increasingly complicated maze of movement-directions. The chaotic jumble of centrifugal line of forces needed to be unified. Simultaneous representation of the numerous visible aspects composing an event was the new representational technique here introduced. The cubist space analysis was synchronized with the line of forces. The body of the moving object, the path of its movement and its background were portrayed in the same picture by fusing all these elements in a kinetic pattern. The romantic language of the futurist manifestos describes the method thus: "The simultaneosity of soul in a work of art; such is the exciting aim of our art. In painting a figure on a balcony, seen from within doors, we shall not confine the view to what can be seen through the frame of the window; we shall give the sum total of the visual sensation of the street, the double row of houses extending right and left the flowered balconies, etc. . . . in other words, a simultaneity of environment and therefore a dismemberment and dislocation of objects, a scattering and confusion of details independent of one and another and without reference to accepted logic," said Marinetti. This concept shows a great similarity to the idea expressed by Einstein, expounding as a physicist the space-time interpretation of the general theory of relativity. "The world of events can be described by a static picture thrown onto the background of the four dimensional time-space continuum. In the past science described motion as happenings in time, general theory of relativity interprets events existing in space-time."

Giacomo Balla. *Dog on Leash 1912.* *Courtesy of The Museum of Modern Art*

Giacomo Balla. *Automobile and Noise.* *Courtesy of Art of This Century*

Marcel Duchamp. *Sad Young Man in a Train.*
Courtesy of Art of This Century

Marcel Duchamp.
Nude Descending the Stairs 1912
Reproduction Courtesy
The Art Institute of Chicago

180

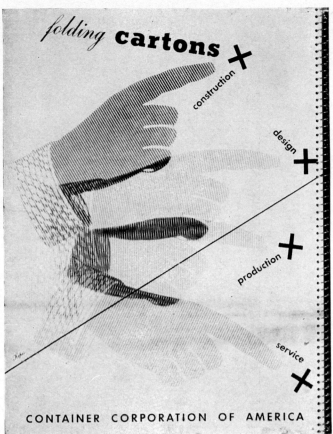

Gyorgy Kepes. *Advertising Design 1938*
Courtesy of Container Corporation of America

Herbert Matter. *Advertising Design*
Courtesy of Container Corporation of America

131

Harold E. Edgerton. *Golfer*

Soviet Poster

E. McKnight Kauffer. *The Early Bird 1919*

Courtesy of The Museum of Modern Art

Delauney. *Circular Rhythm*   *Courtesy of The Guggenheim Museum of Non-Objective Art*

The closest approximation to representation of motion in the genuine terms of the picture-plane was achieved by the utilization of color planes as the organizing factor. The origin of color is light, and colors on the picture surface have an intrinsic tendency to return to their origin. Motion, therefore, is inherent in color. Painters intent on realizing the full motion potentialities of color believed that the image becomes a form only in the progressive interrelationships of opposing colors. Adjacent color-surfaces exhibit contrast effects. They reinforce each other in hue, saturation, and intensity.

The greater the intensity of the color-surfaces achieved by a carefully organized use of simultaneous and successive contrast, the greater their spatial movement color in regard to picture-plane. Their advancing, receding, contracting and circulating movement on the surface creates a rich variety, circular, spiral, pendular, etc., in the process of moulding them into one form which is light or, in practical terms, grey. "Form is movement," declared Delaunay. The classical continuous outline of the objects was therefore eliminated and a rhythmic discontinuity created by grouping colors in the greatest possible contrast. The picture-plane, divided into a number of contrasting color-surfaces of different hue, saturation, and intensity, could be perceived only as a form, as a unified whole in the dynamic sequence of visual perception. The animation of the image they achieved is based upon the progressive steps in bringing opposing colors into balance.

The centrifugal and centripetal forces of the contrasting color-planes move forward and backward, up and down, left and right, compelling the spectator to a kinetic participation as he follows the intrinsic spatial-direction of colors. The dynamic quality is based upon the genuine movement of plastic forces in their tendency toward balance. Like a spinning top or the running wheel of a bicycle, which can find its balance only in movement, the plastic image achieves unity in movement, in perpetual relations of contrasting colors.

A. M. Cassandre. *Poster*

The process of making

The spatial world consists not of instantaneously created units, but of processes of becoming, indefatigable transformations of spatial configurations. Nature forms; flowers, trees, rocks, mountains, cloud formations, animal or human bodies as well as man-made forms; buildings or implements, are only temporarily configurations in the perpetual flux of becoming and disappearing. Every form, therefore, is an inevitable visible record of origin. The spatial configurations of the branches of the trees, the forms of melting metals convey their story of emergence as well as a footstep in the snow or in the sand, the shape of ink spilled from the bottle, or the line pattern drawn by a pencil on a paper. The space-time past—movement—is inherent in every form.

But the space-time background that resulted in a configuration can be so great that it falls beyond the threshold of our ability to grasp it. There are numerous forms in nature whose native history is entirely concealed because the scale of complexity in their origin is too vast. One cannot sense instantaneously in a leaf, in a rock, the kinetic background of their becoming.

 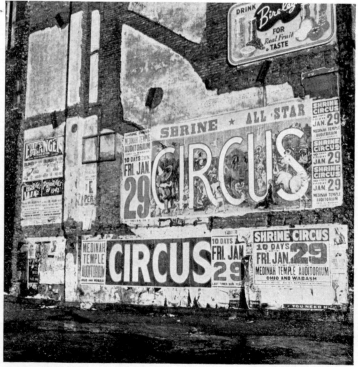

F. Levstik. *Photographs*

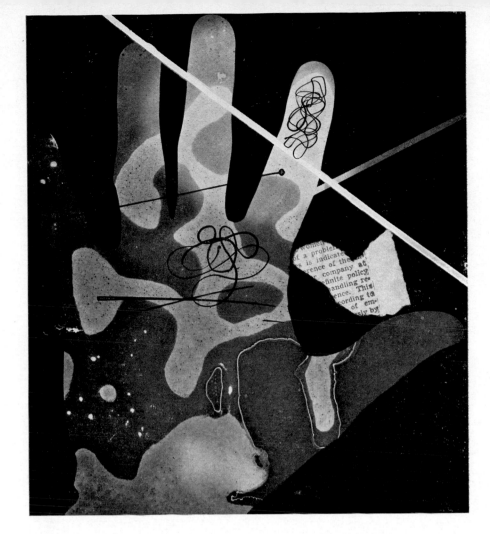

L. Levstik.
Study of Surface Treatment

T. Hauge. Surface Treatment
*Work done for the author's course
in Visual Fundamentals*

*Sponsored by
The Art Director's Club of Chicago*

The material process of making; surface treatment

Making is a spatial activity, and the visible pathway of the movement of a tool on a medium is a spatial message. One cannot avoid seeing, beyond every spatial configuration, the force, the speed and direction of movement which created it. Every created picture image serves, therefore, as an optical expression of movement. The action and the power of the tool, the structure and the texture of the surface resisting the tool, determine the structure of the visible path. Consequently, each tool and each material has its own idiom of movement. The created image is man-made, and here the dynamic spatial background attains a new significance. Making implies body movement. Body movements in turn are evoking a kinetic pleasure, nervous satisfaction. Seeing any man-created visual sign, one unavoidably identifies himself with the maker. One follows the visible tracks of movements and relives again all steps of the neuro-muscular coordination of the original making. A line or a surface suggests the degree of control in its creation. It may have boldness and fluency dictated by the self-confidence of skill, or it may be hesitating, uncontrolled. Thus a line or a surface has an innate kinetic quality independent of what it represents and its plastic relationship on the surface.

Surface-treatment, that is, the visible path of the creative act, determines the genuineness of the expression. In the western culture, representation, with its slavish and obedient portrayal of the object-world, has hampered honest use of the surface-treatment. With meticulous care the painters eliminated all signs of the making. They tried hard to camouflage the fact that the created image is a different reality than the actual subject-matter. In this forgery an important organic quality of the image was lost. In classical art, however, are many examples to prove that its great masters understood the kinetic quality implicit in the surface-treatment. Most of these works were produced at the peak of the painters' development and never became for them standards of pictorial expression. Only contemporary painters through long consistent fight have made surface-treatment an integral factor of visual expression. The same pioneer work which resulted in the liberation of the basic plastic elements, color, planes, and lines, also reclaimed surface-treatment.

The conscious demand for genuine respect of the process of making, however, grew from a more general need than that of the language of vision. Short-sighted profit-hunting — the nineteenth century cannibalism — destroyed almost all living aspects of the work-process, the creative activity. Blind devotion to quantity led to man's enslavement to the machine. The increasing mechanization of production, with all its compulsion of uniformity, rapidly led to the disappearance of real craftsmanship based upon respect for the truth of material, tool, and maker. This shame of the true nature of making, this disregard of the inherent qualities of tools and materials became a dangerous epidemic in every field of human endeavor. From the making of the simplest, every-day object to the widest dimensions of expression, a false attitude was dominant. Not only did it stamp out all rhythmic pleasure in the making, the enjoyment of the work, but it also eclipsed the understanding of the materials and tools. At the early part of the last century Carlyle, and a little later Ruskin and Morris, recognized the devastating consequences of the license of machine-production to creative activity and thus to the life of man. They clearly discerned that the maladjustment of every material and tool man uses implies the maladjustment of man himself. They realized that man must rediscover in every work-process the pleasure of labor, the experience of forming, art, to arrive at an integrated existence. "That thing which I understand by real art is the expression by man of his pleasure in labour. I do not believe he can be happy in his labour without expressing that happiness; . . . A most kind gift is this of nature, since all man, nay, it seems all things, too must labour; . . ." wrote William Morris. This generation faces the task of realizing this vision and extending it on the widest social plane. It is an important task, for it involves not only the revitalization of visual art as such, but even more truly the developing of quickened sensibilities trained to the mission of clearing away falsehood and sham from human relationships.

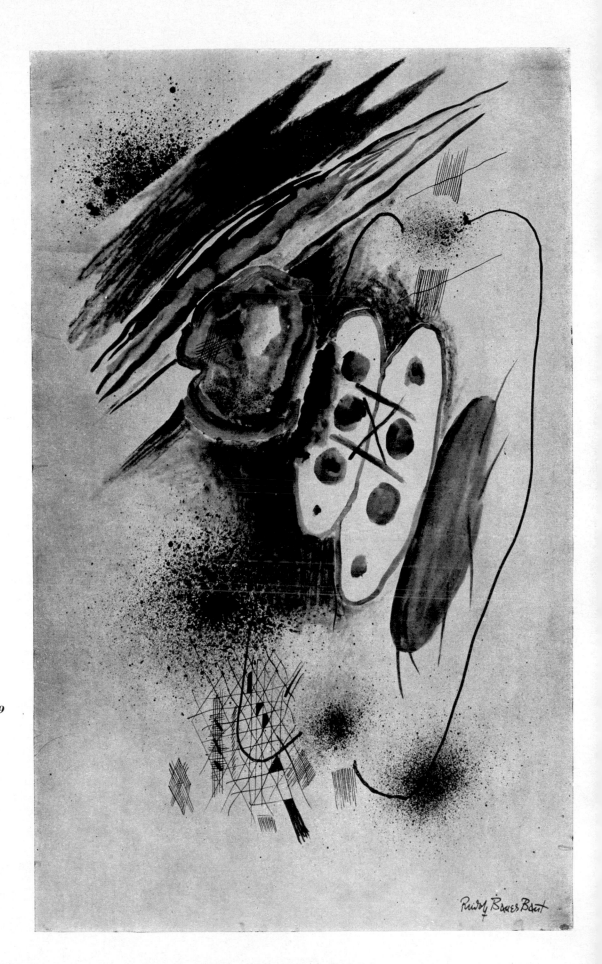

Rudolph Bauer. *Presto 1929*

Courtesy of
The Guggenheim Museum
of Non-Objective Art

189

W. Hogarth.
Dance diagram
Analysis of Beauty

"Nueva Arte de Escribir" By Pedro Diaz Morante Madrid 1626
Courtesy of the Newberry Library

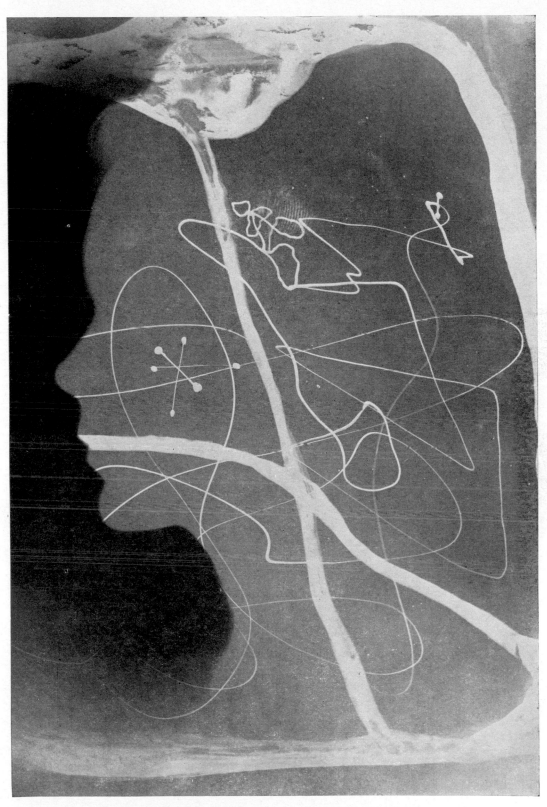

Gyorgy Kepes. *Photogram With Lines 1939*

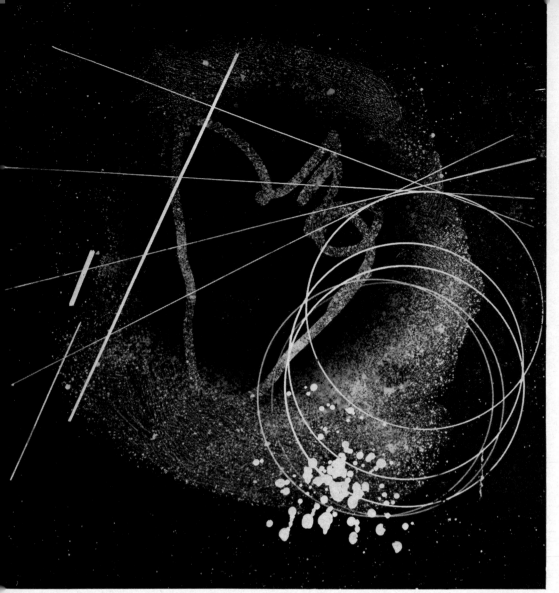

F. Levstik.
Contrasting Surface Treatments

Bobri. *Drawing*

192

As each individual record has its own intrinsic movement-quality—
linear traces evoke an experience of different velocities and rhythm; a
sprayed or printed surface the feeling of an almost instantaneous emerg-
ing—the combination on the same surface of a variety of treatments
creates a visual experience qualified by tension.

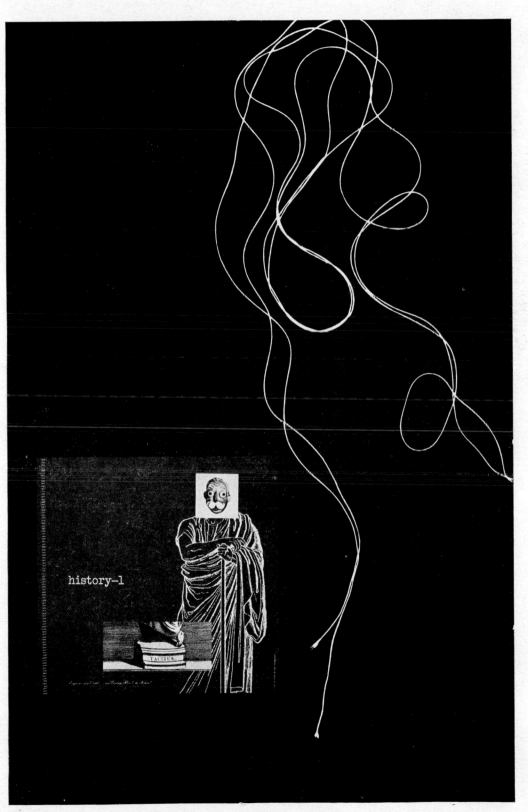

Paul Rand. *Advertising Design*

The psychological process of making

The physical process of making, the execution of the image, is only part of the becoming. Physical tools and medium condition this growth; they do not define its final direction. Man's mind makes the image; his nervous system is the basic tool.

The image grows in the sense that man sees what he wants to see. As each tool has its own unique way of living on the picture surface, so each individual has his own way of binding optical signs into shapes and images he would like to see. As Hans Arp said so convincingly, "Art is a fruit growing out of man, like the fruit out of a plant, like a child out of the mother."

If one looks at a cloud formation, or the pattern made by chance with an ink blot, and finds in them faces, mountains, animals, one creates images which are modelled by unconscious mental processes. The created image, a painting, has similar genesis; it is dictated by emotional necessities, thus stemming from unconscious realms.

One cannot bear chaos in one's psychological space any more than one can bear chaos of the optical impacts of geographical space. Man organizes the optical chaos by forming meaningful spatial wholes. So does he organize the chaos of his psychological space, by forming visual images of his desires, temporary equilibriums in the perpetual conflicts of pleasure and reality; impulses and social taboos. The results of his creative imagination are accepted by him as real forms of his existence. As Freud stated, "Only in one field has the omnipotence of thought been retained in our civilization, namely in art. In art alone it still happens that man, consumed by his wishes, produces something similar to the gratification of these wishes, and this playing, thanks to artistic illusion, calls forth effects as if it were something real."

The same social events that caused the draining of the rhythm—the pleasure of making—from the physical process of making also sapped the internal process of making of its most essential nourishment. The static object concept, the fixed perspective of the psychological space, froze the biomorphic rhythm of visual imagery. The fetish of our time—the mechanical manufactured commodity—stamped its pattern on the creative process. It was not by accident that one of the first rebels against the wrongs of the industrial revolution, Carlyle, wrote in 1831, "The artificial is the conscious mechanical; the natural is the unconscious, dynamical. Unconsciousness is the sign of creation; consciousness at best that of manufacture." Today the protest has taken vehement form. Contemporary artists, revolting against the fetters of static concept, throw away all conscious control. Artistic endeavour was reduced, only to a sheer assistance of chance happenings. The artist acts the role of the midwife. He only assists at the birth of a living form that grows from deeper strata than his conscious efforts could reach. He invents techniques that give the fewest obstacles to the free flow of organic formation.

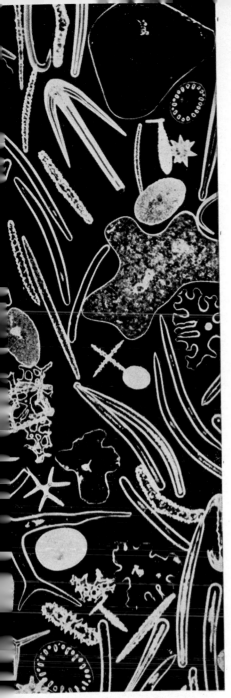

Hans Arp cut out bits of colored paper and, with deliberate abandon, tossed them on a piece of cardboard, threw them around, and finally turned them over and pasted on the cardboard the pattern that they formed by chance. Such chance has in it, however, more reason than we, with our present blinkers and confused senses, can see. The resulting order shows an organic understanding far more embracing than the formal logic-sharpened-in-static-object concept. It is natural that these automatic expressions resemble the biomorphic realms of nature. They have the same order as the visible forms of mutations, transformations, the perpetual asymmetric rhythm of the processes not yet fossilized in terms of things.

Hans Arp. _Mountain, Table, Anchors, Navel 1925_
Courtesy of The Museum of Modern Art

Microphotograph
of Sponge Spicules

195

Ink Blots

Plastic thinking, thinking with the senses, stated the desires and the will of men opposed to machine control. Having achieved the scientific mastery of a new vast territory of nature and its ordering into a one-sided technological dimension, man was searching for renewed contact with the pulsation of the dynamic forces of nature processes. He recognized that scientific technological progress needed to be revaluated in biological dimensions. Instead of the old fixed point of perspective, he developed, to meet his need, the perspective of growth instead of static order, the dynamic rhythm. The artist rediscovered nature. But he turned away from the naturalistic representation of the forms of the trees, flowers, and animals, and took as his new subject-matter the visible processes of the growth.

Juan Miro.
Dutch Interior 1928
Courtesy of Art of This Century

Paul Klee. *Male and Female Plant 1921*
Courtesy of Art of This Century

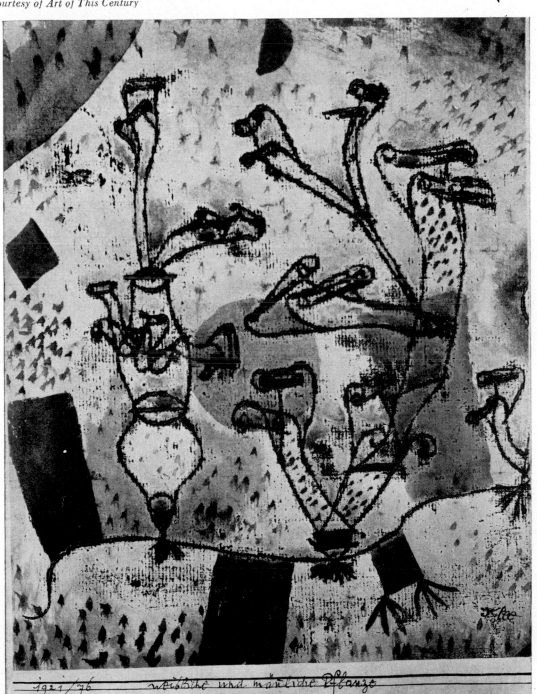

1921/76   weibliche und männliche Pflanze

Herbert Bayer. *Messages Through The Atmosphere 1942*

Herbert Bayer. *Painting 1942*

Joseph Feher. *Advertising Design*

Paul Rand. *Advertising Design*

summer...

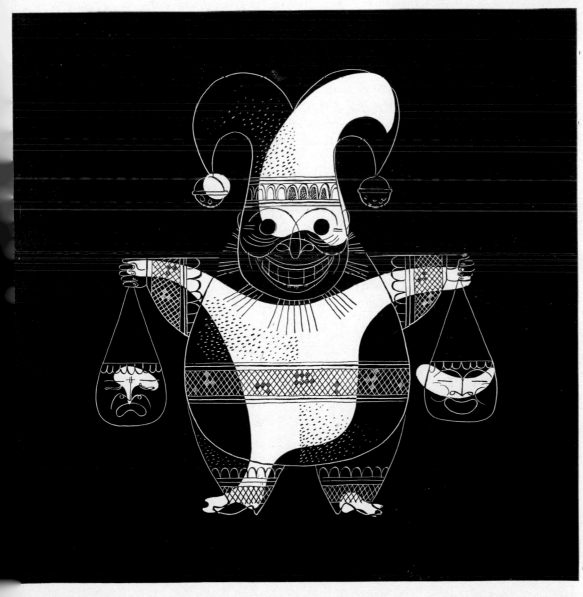

Toward a dynamic iconography

Visual experience is more than the experience of pure sensory qualities. Visual sensations are interwoven with memory overlays. Each visual configuration contains a meaningful text, evokes associations of things, events; creates emotional and conscious responses.

Literary imitation of nature tied to a fixed point of observation had killed the image as a plastic organism. It was quite natural, therefore, that the associative meaning should be identified with the literary content and hence disposed of as unnecessary. Non-representational art clarified the structural laws of the plastic image. It reestablished the image in its original role as a dynamic experience based upon the properties of the senses and their plastic organization. But it threw overboard the meaningful signs of the visual relationships.

The image was "purified." But this purification overlooked the fact that the distortion and disintegration of the image as a plastic experience had not been due to represented meaningful signs as such but rather to the prevailing representation-concept which was static and limited, and consequently in contradiction to the dynamic plastic nature of the visual experience. The structure of meaning had been based upon the same conception which generated the fixed point of view of space representation, linear perspective and modelling by shading. Things had been represented together in a fixed system of empirical order and their meaning also had acquired the characteristic of this fixity.

Juan Gris, one of the foremost of the painters working toward the new language of vision, made it clear that new, healthy plastic structure is not an ultimate goal, but only a new start toward the understanding of values inherent in the relationships of the meaningful elements of visible nature. "I try to give concrete form to what is abstract, I pass from the general to the particular, by which I mean that I take abstraction as my point of departure and the real fact as my point of arrival . . . I consider mathematics to be the architectural side of painting, the abstract side, and I want to humanize it; Cezanne makes a cylinder of a bottle, I began with the cylinder in order to create an individual unit of special type. Of a cylinder I make a bottle, a particular bottle. Cezanne works toward architecture, I work away from it; that is why I compose with abstractions, (in color) and I arrange when these colors have become objects; for example I compose with a white and black and I arrange when the white has become a paper, and that black a shadow! I mean to say that I arrange the white to make it become a paper and the black to make it become a shadow."

Whitehead, one of the leading scholars of today, understands this when he writes:

"Thus 'art' in the general sense which I require, is any selection by which the concrete facts are so arranged as to elicit attention to particular values which are realizable by them. For example, the mere disposal of the human body and the eyesight, so as to get a good view of a sunset is a simple form of artistic selection. The habit of art is the habit of enjoying vivid values."[•]

What are these values? What are the concrete facts? Value is, stated very generally, that which renders anything useful. Values are, in human terms, the recognized directives toward a more satisfactory human life. They are the comprehended potential "order" in man's relationship to nature and to his fellow men. Order makes sense only as an order in a definite field. Values are conditioned by concrete events of the physical, psychological and social realms. Values have not yet been formulated for our time. We are living in a formless age of transition, of chaos, incomparable to anything man has ever experienced before. In this confusion, plastic art, the most direct experience of order, the forming activity par excellence, gains significance. Order for our time can only be formulated in the concrete terms of the dynamic field of the present social forces. Only if we encompass in thinking and in seeing the dynamic forces the present contradictions in biological and social processes, shall we be able to resolve them. Only if we can guide the events of our time toward "planned," integrated social organization, can we reach a new temporary equilibrium; a more satisfactory human life.

Thinking and seeing, in terms of static, isolated things identical only with themselves, have an initial inertia which cannot keep pace with the stride of life, thus cannot suggest values—plastic order—intrinsic in this dynamic field of social existence. Common sense regards rest and motion as entirely different processes. Yet rest is, in reality, a special kind of motion, and motion is, in a sense, a kind of rest. The plastic image can fulfill its present social mission only by encompassing this identity of opposing directions and referring it to concrete social experiences. Inherited visual language has fossilized the events in a static sign system. Revolution in the plastic arts has brought back a dynamic approach on the sensory level. The plastic structures must expand to absorb, without giving up their plastic strength, the meaningful images of current concrete social experiences. The task of the contemporary artist is to release and bring into social action the dynamic forces of visual imagery. As contemporary scientists are struggling to liberate the arrested energy of the atom, painters of our day must liberate the inexhaustible energy reservoir of the visual associations. To accomplish this, they need a clear grasp of the social field, intellectual honesty, and creative power capable of integrating experiences into a plastic form. This goal will be reached only when art once more lives in inseparable unity with human life.

[•] *Whitehead, Science and the Modern World*

Each representation of an object or a thing acts on the picture surface and discharges its own unique direction of associations as a point, a line, a shape, acts on the picture-plane, and forces the eye into virtual spatial directions. These representations have positions, direction, shape, size, distance, and weight. They can advance until one is keen to follow them, or they can recede so that one is willing to miss them. They have textures of sensory warmth; or they are cold, with geometrical or theoretical exactness. They have brightness and color and can move with various velocities. As one searches for spatial order, and through the interrelationships of the plastic forces creates a unified spatial whole, one also searches for a meaning-order and builds from the different association-directions the common, meaningful whole.

We look at a photograph of two men sitting on a bench, and each unit of the picture brings up associations. One man is better dressed than the other. They are sitting back to back. Their bodies, their postures are full of associative suggestions. We compare them and contrast them, discovering differences and similarities. We try to bridge the differences by use of the similarities. The image becomes a dynamic experience. It has a self-movement because of the discovered opposition. The experience attains a unity as we fill out, with a living story, the latent human background of the visible situation. We do not see things, fixed static units, but perceive instead living relationships. We look at the photograph of an eye stuck in mud and see in the same picture barbed-wire. The contradiction inherent in the associations of the respective elements keeps our mind moving until the contradiction is resolved in a meaning; until that meaning, in turn, becomes an attitude toward things around us and serves as ferment for protest against life under inhuman conditions. Contradiction is then the basis of dynamic organization of the associative qualities of the image. When representational units within the same picture contain statements which seem counter to the accepted logic of events, the spectator's attention is forced to seek out the possible relationships until a central idea is found which weaves the meaningful signs together in a meaningful whole. The association-fields of the representation of a man, a tree, a machine, and so on, in their combination on a picture surface, can reinforce one another or clash with one another, creating strains, stresses, tensions. Each tension is resolved into a meaning configuration. These configurations in turn serve as a basis for further tensions; consequently for further configurations. Meaningful signs have thus their laws of organization similar to the plastic organization. But whereas the relationship of plastic qualities emerges through the dynamic organization of the spectator into a spatial whole, in the case of organization of meaningful signs the unifying whole has the dimensions of human attitudes, feeling and thought.

F. Levstik. *Photograph*

N. Lerner. *Eye and Barbed Wire*

It was pointed out before that the line of our communication into the dynamic background of association was cut by a short-circuit when picture elements were presented in static correspondence with the things they represented, when the representation of things and the things themselves were considered identical. The path led then, not to progressive, evolving discovery of the relationships of things, but only to things themselves and their associative meanings. On a weak plastic foundation, it became progressively dangerous to build a structure of associations referring to concrete feelings and values. But after painters had tested and rebuilt the plastic foundation, visual expression went ahead to use this structure for redirecting us to the plastic order—the meaningful order—in the life man makes for himself.

The stages of development through which the structural use of associations has passed correspond to those in the search for the laws of plastic organization. Meaning-unity was first disintegrated into meaning-facets. Later, these meaning-facets were understood in their interconnections, evaluated as forces and fields, tested in their tensions, dynamic equilibrium, and reorganized into a new meaningful whole.

Disintegration of the fixed system of meaning organization

The disintegration was provoked by the social contradictions in which man was living. At the end of the last war, in revolt against an apparently hopeless mess of political and cultural frustration, against the piracy of mediocrity, fake values, and false authority, men eagerly discarded every value, and thus every meaning. Artists, no less than other men, lost their belief in the meaningfulness of their own lives and of life in general. In blind hate they set forth to destroy everything which contained the smallest kernel of meaningful coherency. Social institutions, customs, ethical or moral values, feelings and works of art were, they declared, a perpetuation of the old nonsense—a cancer in human existence. They saw about them evidences of tremendous, painstaking effort in the creation of works of art whose final results were devoid of social meaning. They attacked, therefore, fiercely and without discrimination, the meaning-structure of art. With bitter irony, they took fragments as their plastic raw material: the rubbish of the wastebasket, newspapers, streetcar tickets, blotting-paper, old buttons, torn photographs, postcards. But they could not rid themselves of the instinctive desire to form, to mould a plastic order. They bound together all these fragments which were taken from their context and had no logical connection whatsoever, and this random conglomeration of unrelated, fragmentary signs of meaningful pictures revealed an unexpected power of expression.

Kurt Schwitters. *Relief Merzbild 1915*
Courtesy of Art of This Century

Each material, each shape, each photograph carried within itself characteristics of the world from which it was taken. The observer was forced to find order in the unrelated fragments, to trace back some latent meaningful connections in the basically meaningless haphazard dada and merz-pictures, collages or photomontages. The wider apart the elements were in meaning and the more impossible it seemed to find integration for them, the greater became the tension of the spectator as he struggled to find a source of integration. This tension was a zero point of the meaning-organization. It served as a basis for redirection.

Harold Walter. *Collage* •

M. Martin Johnson. *Collage* •

*• Work done for the author's course in Visual Fundamentals
Sponsored by the Art Director's Club of Chicago, 1938*

Just as, after the disintegration of fixed Renaissance perspective, lines and color-planes had revealed a dynamic quality and had moved in every spatial direction, so after the disintegration of the fixed meaning-unity of traditional logic, associative energies inherent in every visible fragment of reality were suddenly released. The next step was made toward the reintegration of these liberated meaning-facets.

The new tendency—and to a great degree its results—was not so new as it appeared. As the revolutionary innovations in spatial representation had rediscovered the original basis of the image, the researches in the handling of "subject matter" and the dynamic ordering of the meaning element reestablished an old basic principle of creative expression, the freedom of expression from one-sided naturalism. It reaffirmed this principle with hitherto undared consistency. It reinforced the bloodless primitive symbolic iconography with a sensory dynamic basis of plastic organization. It evaluated allegory, the static balance of meaningful signs, into a dynamic equilibrium.

There were many convergent directions in these attempts to bind the liberated meaning-facets into a new dynamic whole. Painting enriched with new idioms, collage and photomontage, contributed toward the structural understanding of the relationship of representational signs, and cleared the way for this redirection. The motion picture made the first thorough analysis of the structural connection of representational images in actual time sequence. Advertising art pioneered in testing representational images in combination with pure plastic units and verbal elements.

Mexican Picture Postcard.

Giuseppe Arcimboldo. *Summer*
Reproduction Courtesy
The Art Institute of Chicago

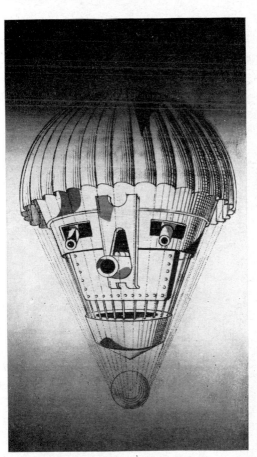

Xanti Schawinsky. *War*

207

G. Apollinaire. *Ideogram*

Gyorgy Kepes. *Stalingrad 1942*

Apollinaire in his ideograms, Miro in his painting-poem incorporate the written word in the plastic ensemble with a dynamic interaction of the verbal significance and the sensory qualities of the pictorial elements. These painters are fusing the two into one expression that evokes associations of great depth because of the sensory intensity of plastic values, and of great width because of the associations discharged by the linguistic basis. Color, shape, and texture, line, and symbol attain an organic unity and thus train the spectator to form into an organic whole his own experiences of the divergent qualities.

We have seen that the image becomes a living experience on the sensory level only through dynamic participation of the beholder. We saw that plastic experience is based upon the dynamic tendency of the beholder, who cannot bear chaos, cannot bear contradiction, and consequently searches for order, for a unified whole which can bind the apparently opposing or contradicting virtual spatial directions of the visual units into a spatial unity. A similar dynamic participation also brings about the integration of meaningful visual signs.

The living fibre of our unconscious responses is given by the concrete images of the surrounding events. Visual expression, based upon the understanding of the dynamic structure of the visual imagery, can be invaluable in readjusting our thinking as a dynamic process. When the plastic organization and the organization of the meaningful signs are synchronized into a common dynamic structure, we have a significant implement of progress. Such images suggest a new thinking-habit, reinforced with the elementary strength of sensory experience. From them the nervous system can acquire the new discipline necessary to the dynamics of contemporary life.

The consequences of social chaos finally penetrated into the most sheltered regions of individual life. Maladjusted man lost his grip in keeping in the background the dynamic events in his psychological space. Destructive sex impulses, fear of death and the unknown which were domesticated by dreams and mythology in more integrated cultures, lost their masters, and, running amok, invaded the conscious domains. It could no longer be denied that the subconscious is the real background of psychological events and that the conscious, using Freud's comparison, is like the visible small fraction of an iceberg, of which the larger part has its menacing existence submerged under the sea.

Scientific advance and advancing optical mastery of reality again went along converging avenues. The process of understanding physical space was repeated in psychological space. In science, the Euclidian geometry was recognized as only the first approximation of space and in painting the fixed perspective as an insufficient rendering of spatial experiences. In psychology, the conscious region was understood as only a limited complex of psychological events, and its representation in art as only the first step of its creative expression. And as the pioneer scientists found a "more real" picturing of the physical space by fusing space and time into one indivisible unity, and pioneer painters a "more real" representation by welding objects and background into a dynamic plastic unity by interpenetration of color planes and lines, so the pioneers of the psychological space searched for "a more real world than the real behind the real," by fusion of the conscious and subconscious experiences; in Andre Breton's words: "the future resolution of the two states (in appearance contradictory), dream and reality, into a sort of absolute reality." The object that had been analyzed by the cubist painters in the background of the space-time field, was now being analyzed by the surrealist painters in the field of the subconscious associations. "It is essentially upon the objects that surrealism has thrown most light in recent years. Only the very close examination of the many recent speculations to which the object has publicly given rise (the oneric object, the object functioning symbolically, the phantom object, the discovered object, etc.), can give one a proper grasp of the experiments that surrealism is engaged in now," said Andre Breton in "What Is Surrealism."

The subconscious, manifested in dreams and free associations, has another logic than that of space-time derived from empirical facts, and the new picture-image, in a sovereign automatism, brought together representation of objects unrelated in the everyday experiences. But the importance of one or another object in the frustrated subconscious sphere dictated its size and position on the picture surface. The structure of the associative content dominated the picture organization. Consequently, the plastic order was again restricted.

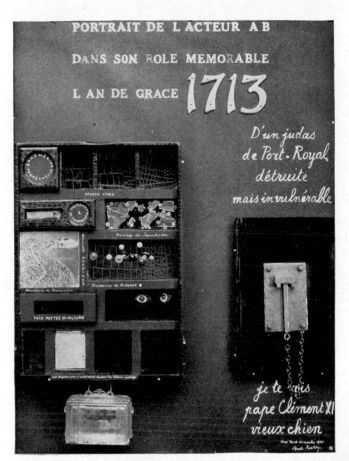

Andre Breton. *Portrait of An Actor A. B. 1941*
Courtesy of Art of This Century

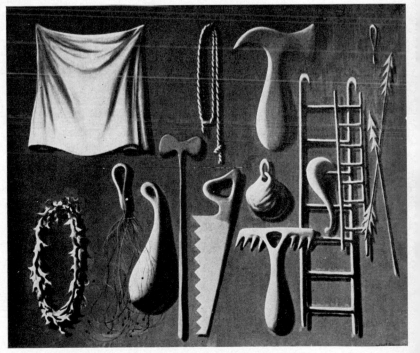

Herbert Bayer. *Deposition 1940*

Max Ernst. Painting
Courtesy of Art of This Century

Marc Chagall. *Paris Through The Window 1912*
Courtesy of The Museum of Modern Art

Francis Picabia. *Very Rare Picture Upon Earth*

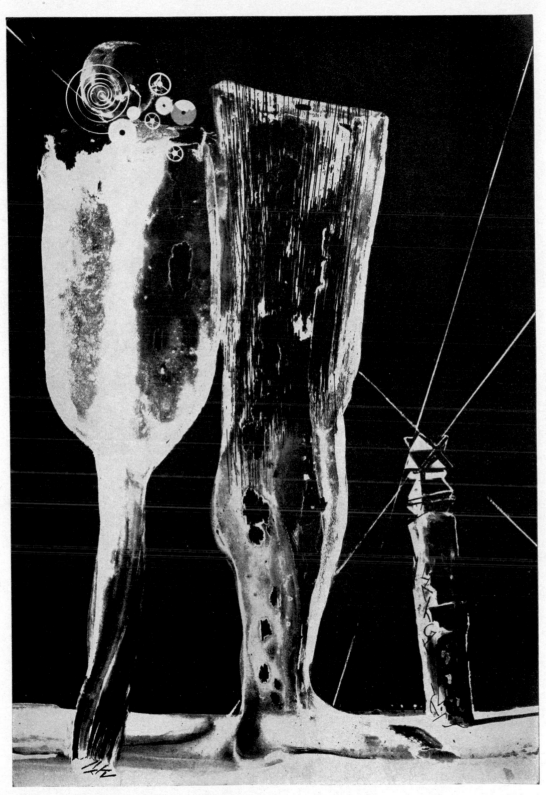

Gyorgy Kepes. *Hungarian Past. Photogram*

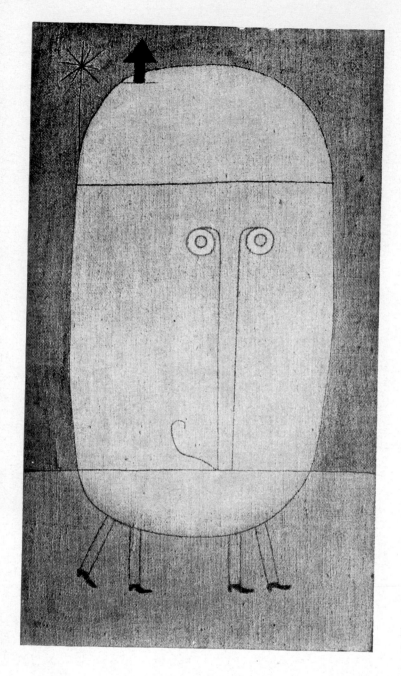

Paul Klee. *Mask of Fear*
Courtesy of The Museum of Modern Art

Some visual expressions, however, did approximate the goal of synchronizing the plastic structure with images of concrete social events. Though their range and importance are on different levels, they indicate a new path for visual expression. Picasso, stirred to a fury of indignation by a human drama caused by the regressive social forces and their significance today, in a visual projection of the discrepancy between life as it is and life as it should be, represents human figures in a distortion of pain and suffering. Mouth and lips, nose and nostrils, are shaped by pain in positions far from empirical reality and yet close enough so that they are recognizable in familiar terms. Tears are in action like a bursting bomb. The plastic interconnection of the lines, planes, and texture-surfaces acts as do suffering individuals. Lines try to escape from the picture surface, running with an incredible optical fury; planes follow each other in a rhythmic sequence resembling the shrieks of a danger siren. Textures break up the surface like bayonets tearing a living body. But all these violent plastic forces are organized as a visual progression in which each part demands the other, and can live only through the help of the other. One shape takes over the direction of another shape; one tone value repeats or contrasts a foregoing value in the living rhythm of an integrated whole. Two contradicting systems, plastic-organization—the message of order—and the organization of a meaningful whole—the message of chaos—are welded in an indivisible whole.

Picasso. *Guernica*
Reproduction Courtesy The Art Institute of Chicago

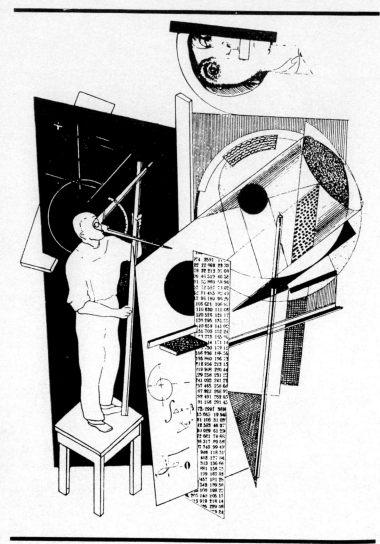

Moholy Nagy. *Leda. Photomontage 1926*

Technological motivations. The invention of photomontage

The complexity of machine culture confronted man's vision with serious obstacles. Machines and many machine products cannot be understood from their exterior image alone. A machine is a functioning, moving unit. The only adequate way to master it visually is to perceive it in its dynamic quality, in the functioning interconnections of its visible parts. Naturalistic photography, with its traditional fixed point of view, could not represent it. Most of the new technical units were commodities to sell; optical sales-talk, therefore, needed to make use of the simultaneous projections. And long before painters began to attack the problem, advertising in this country was already making use of the photomontage. The solution resembled the cubist analysis of space, but it had this difference; whereas in cubist paintings the connectedness of the elements was dictated by the aim of making the object clear in all visible spatial aspects, in the photomontage that connectedness was dictated by the functional, meaningful relationships of the represented object-elements.

The idea of dissecting and rearranging photographic elements and combining them with drawings was carried further in the experimental forms of photomontage. Like an interaction of cogwheels, space was represented by the interaction of lines and shapes without naturalistic references and by photographic and drawn units with fragments of the familiar spatial aspects. The resulting image produces a dynamic spatial experience by the coordination of representations of actual three-dimensional units and pure plastic elements of lines and shapes.

Ruth Robbins. *Montage*

Work done for the Author's course in Visual Fundamentals *School of Design in Chicago*

Clifford Eitel.
Photomontage.

Elsa Kula Pratt.
Photomontage.

*Work done for the Author's course
in Visual Fundamentals
School of Design in Chicago*

All these findings came to focus in the practical tasks of contemporary advertising art. Advertising could utilize them because it was not handicapped by traditional forms. Advertising was made to utilize them because it belonged to its very nature to be contemporary and forceful, and it could be so only through the use of the new dynamic visual idioms. A sheer illustration of a fact or of an idea was not vital enough to induce strong responses in the spectator. To put an advertising message through effectively, the most heterogeneous elements—verbal message, drawing, photography and abstract shapes—were employed. This variety of meaningful signs and symbols could only be integrated by a dynamic meaning organization. Visual advertising, however, has the eye as its customer. To satisfy this customer, it must be vital as a visual experience and it must offer comfort to the eye. Each meaningful unit has an optical basis. It has color, value, texture, shape, direction, size and interval. Advertising for its well-conceived interest learned to use the dynamic plastic organization of these optical qualities; that is, it became an art. Here lies a great challenge for advertising today. Contemporary man-made environment makes up a very large part of man's visible surroundings. Posters on the streets, picture magazines, picture books, container labels, window displays, and innumerable other existing or potential forms of visual publicity could then serve a double purpose. They could disseminate socially useful messages, and they could train the eye, and thus the mind, with the necessary discipline of seeing beyond the surface of visible things, to recognize and enjoy values necessary for an integrated life. If social conditions allow advertising to serve messages that are justified in the deepest and broadest social sense, advertising art could contribute effectively in preparing the way for a positive popular art, an art reaching everybody and understood by everyone.

Morton Goldsholl. *Advertising Design 1943*

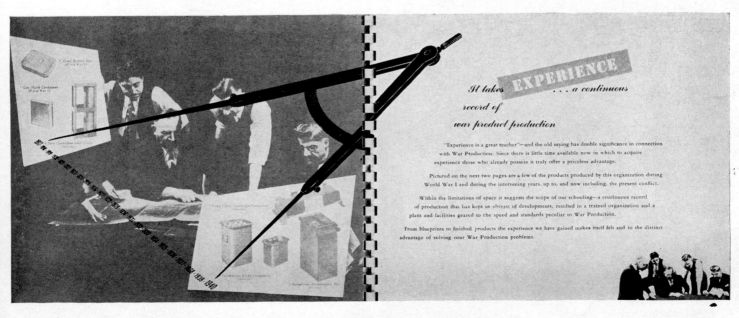

Herbert Bayer. *Advertising Design 1943*

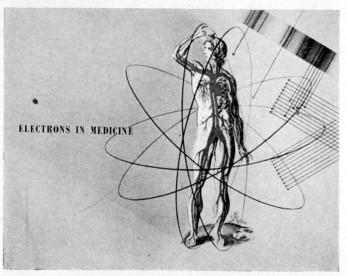

Herbert Bayer. *Advertising Design 1943*

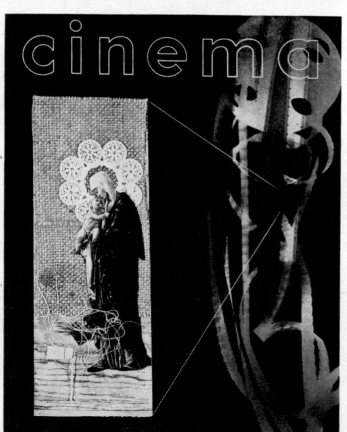

Harold Walter. *Collage 1938*

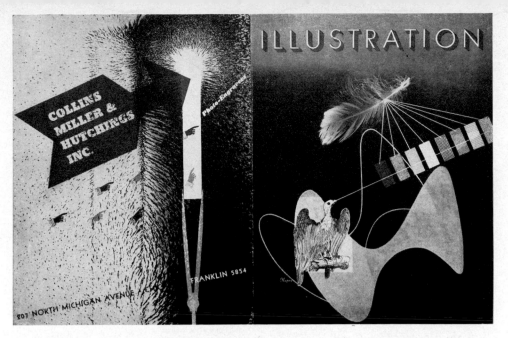

Gyorgy Kepes. *Cover Design*
Courtesy of Collins, Miller & Hutchings Inc.

Gyorgy Kepes. *Advertising Design*
Courtesy of Collins, Miller & Hutchings Inc.

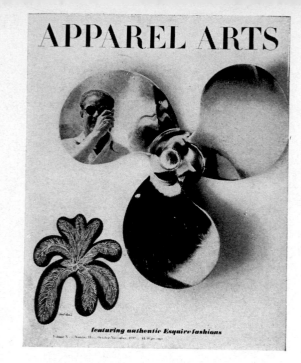

Paul Rand. *Cover Design*

W. Burtin. *Advertising Design 1941*

Alexei Brodovich. *Poster 1942*

Joseph Feher. *Advertising Design*
Courtesy of Collins, Miller & Hutchings Inc.

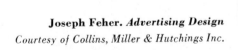

"YOU PAYS YOUR MONEY AND YOU TAKES YOUR CHOICE"

In his Informal History of the New Orleans Underworld, Herbert Asbury points out that innumerable books and articles have proved conclusively that Jean Lafitte was a pirate, a murderer, and a great villain; other books and articles just as numerous have proved just as conclusively that

M. Lafitte, was no pirate at all, but a staunch patriot, a gentleman smuggler, a much misunderstood man. As the Louisiana darkies say, "You pays your money and you takes your choice."

When you buy engravings, you also—"pays your money and you takes your choice." When you buy your engravings from Collins, Miller & Hutchings, however, there is no choice. You always get the finest engravings we know how to make at a price that is the same to all.

225

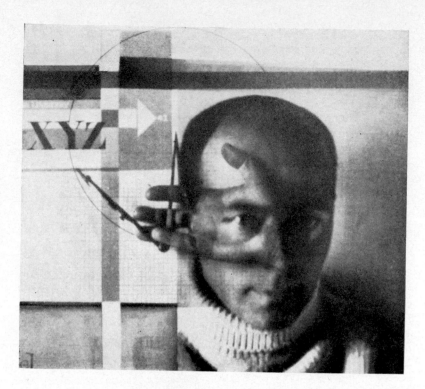

El Lissitzky. *Self Portrait 1924*

Herbert Bayer. *Advertising Design 1939*

A. M. Cassandre. *Poster 1925*
Courtesy of The Museum of Modern Art

Jean Carlu. *Poster 1940*